"*Twenty years working in television news has enabled me to recognize a powerful story when I see one. Kent Whitaker tells a remarkable first-person account of love and unimaginable family betrayal that puts his faith to the ultimate test. His gut-wrenching moral dilemma will have you asking, 'What would I do?'*"

—**Jay Young,** Edward R. Murrow Award winner, and two-time Emmy-winning producer, CBS News

"Murder by Family *is an achingly human exploration of the dynamics of forgiveness. It might be the most poignant book on the subject since Simon Wiesenthal's* The Sunflower."

—**Donald Miller,** author, *Blue Like Jazz*

"*Kent's story is amazing and inspiring! There is no better legacy that Kent can leave than his story of forgiveness and love.*"

—**Pat Nolan,** vice president, Prison Fellowship Ministries

"Murder by Family *is a captivating, heart-wrenching, emotion-evoking journey of a father who is betrayed by a son he deeply loves. This book reads like a novel, but grips the heart with tenacity because it's the true story of a man who loses the people he loves most and then willfully chooses to forgive the perpetrator. Kent Whitaker writes with vulnerability, honesty, and passion. My heart beats with his. My own son is a murderer. I know this pain. I understand the depth of this love.* Murder by Family *will capture your heart and challenge you to be a person who forgives.*"

—**Carol Kent,** speaker and author, *When I Lay My Isaac Down* and *A New Kind of Normal*

MURDER

BY FAMILY

*The Incredible True Story
of a Son's Treachery
and
a Father's Forgiveness*

KENT WHITAKER

HOWARD BOOKS
A DIVISION OF SIMON & SCHUSTER

New York   London   Toronto   Sydney

Our purpose at Howard Books is to:
- *Increase faith* in the hearts of growing Christians
- *Inspire holiness* in the lives of believers
- *Instill hope* in the hearts of struggling people everywhere

Because He's coming again!

Published by Howard Books,
a division of Simon & Schuster, Inc.
1230 Avenue of the Americas, New York, NY 10020
www.howardpublishing.com

Murder by Family © 2008 Kent Whitaker

Published in association with Janet Kobobel Grant
and the literary agency of Books & Such, Inc.

Library of Congress Cataloging-in-Publication Data is available.

ISBN 978-1-4165-7813-0
ISBN 978-1-4391-6460-0 (pbk)
ISBN 978-1-4391-3998-1 (ebook)

10 9 8 7 6 5 4 3 2 1

HOWARD and colophon are registered trademarks
of Simon & Schuster, Inc.

Manufactured in the United States of America

For information regarding special discounts for bulk purchases,
please contact Simon & Schuster Special Sales at
1-866-506-1949 or business@simonandschuster.com.

The Simon & Schuster Speakers Bureau can bring authors to your
live event. For more information or to book an event, contact the
Simon & Schuster Speakers Bureau at 1-866-248-3049 or
visit our website at www.simonspeakers.com.

Edited by Between the Lines

Quote by Max Lucado reprinted by permission. *Everyday Blessings*, Max Lucado,
copyright 2004, Thomas Nelson, Inc., Nashville, Tennessee. All rights reserved.

Excerpt from *The Adventures of the Stainless Steel Rat*, copyright © 1978
by Harry Harrison. Used by permission.

In loving memory of Tricia and Kevin

Contents

It is not our ability to think that separates us from the lower animals. It is our capacity to repent and to forgive that makes us different.

—*Aleksandr Solzhenitsyn*

To forgive someone is to admit our limitations. We've been given only one piece of life's jigsaw puzzle. Only God has the cover of the box.

—*Max Lucado*, Everyday Blessings

In the Bible we read that King David's darkest hour was upon hearing that his son Absalom was dead. Absalom had killed his brother, plotted to take David's throne, and raised an army whose main goal was to kill David in battle. Yet David loved and forgave his son, crying bitter tears at the news of his death.

A thousand years later, Jesus told the story of another foolish young man who rejected and abandoned his father, running away to a foreign land. Jesus used this parable of the prodigal son to show us the unconditional love and forgiveness God has for all of his wayward children and to illustrate how he will patiently wait for us to come to our senses and return to him. As in the story of David and Absalom, the father in the parable did not ignore or remove the consequences of his son's actions; but he did forgive those actions, just as God will restore and forgive all repentant prodigals.

This is the story of a modern-day father whose life was torn apart by his own Absalom. It is the true story of a dad who slowly came to recognize the truth of his son's guilt yet stubbornly refused to abandon him, even in the face of horrible testimony. Instead of condemnation, he offered the grace and forgiveness that Jesus calls us to extend to all who hurt us. It is the story of a father's dawning realization that his son had secretly moved into darkness, scheming to take his life—and of how prayer, forgiveness, and faith brought their winding roads back together and into the light.

It is a modern-day participation in David's tears, and a living-out of the old parable.

It is my story.

Chapter 1

THE FIRST 200 MINUTES

I had always heard that your life flashed before your eyes. But that's not what happened as I lay on the cold concrete that December night, watching the blood from a gunshot wound cover my white shirt. Instead, I found myself praying for my family. There had been four shots, one for each of us.

I told God that if it was my time, I was ready to die, but I prayed that he would spare my wife and two sons. I called to each of them but got no response except for a few quiet, wet coughs from my wife, Tricia. Although I couldn't see her from where I had fallen, I knew that it was her because when I had first tried to get up, I saw her blond hair splayed out on the threshold of our home's front door. Though I had never heard that kind of cough before, I instinctively knew it was the sound of a person trying to clear lungs filling with blood. The silence coming from the dark house was horrible. *My God, I thought, he's shot us all.*

Life can change in a moment. Just seconds earlier we had been a happy family of four returning from a surprise dinner celebrating our older son Bart's anticipated college graduation. He had called that afternoon, telling Tricia that he was through with exams and was coming home for the evening. We had enjoyed a great seafood dinner, including a dessert with "Congratulations!" written with chocolate syrup on the plate's edge. I snapped a few pictures, and then we took the short drive home. How strange that those would be the last photos we would ever have together.

As we got out of the car, our younger son, Kevin, a sophomore in college, led the way to our front door. He stepped inside, with Tricia right behind him. I heard a huge noise, but I didn't immediately recognize it as a gunshot. A moment of silence, and then Tricia exclaimed, "Oh, no!" as another shot was fired. I still didn't understand what was happening. I stepped forward and for the first time saw inside the house. The light from the front porch illuminated a ski-masked figure about eight feet away, standing next to the stairs. I couldn't see Kevin, though he was lying in the shadows next to where the man was standing—or Tricia, who must have been right by my feet. I just stood there wondering which one of Kevin's goofball friends was playing a joke on us with the paintball gun.

Suddenly I was slammed in the shoulder with enough force to send me spinning back and to my left. Landing faceup on the front porch, I still didn't grasp what was happening. As I tried to get up, I felt a searing pain in my right arm and realized it was badly broken. A fourth shot rang out as comprehension flooded in. We had been shot. We had all been shot. It struck me that I might be dying.

Then my neighbor Cliff was kneeling over me, comforting me. "Don't worry, buddy! Help is on the way!"

In the distance I heard sirens as Cliff pulled off his T-shirt and pressed it to my wound. I realized then that no one knew where the shooter was and that Cliff might be in danger. I panicked. "Get out of here! He may still be inside!"

Cliff told me to hold on and ran home. Moments later a squad car pulled up in front of our house, and then another, and a third. I was aware of more sirens, including the deep foghorn of a fire truck, but they were still far away. With heightened senses I heard muffled footfalls as police ran into and around the house, guns drawn and flashlights flicking illumination into the shadows. After only a minute or two someone called out that the house was clear. By then the whole cul-de-sac that faced our home was full of emergency vehicles. It couldn't have been more than five minutes since the shootings.

People were everywhere. Neighbors were streaming out of their homes while paramedics swarmed. Two men worked on me, cutting away my leather jacket and my shirt, trying to stop the bleeding. I repeatedly asked for information on my family, and finally one of the paramedics quietly said, "Sir, please, let us do our job. You're in good hands, and lots of good folks are with the rest of your family."

Then, over all the confusion and noise, as they hurried inside the house, I heard one policeman ask another, "What do you want to do about the DOA?"

My heart froze. Dead on arrival. I knew that at least one of my family members had died. But which one? And why? Were they all dead?

The sound of a helicopter cut through the night, and I saw the landing lights and then the cherry-red body of Life Flight. Three paramedics raced a gurney down the sidewalk, and one of the police officers told me that they were taking Tricia to the hospital. My heart leaped with joy, because that meant she was still alive. Thank God! But then I realized that this also meant that at least one, and by now perhaps both, of my boys were dead. I began to shake all over and knew I was going into shock. I chattered to the paramedics that I was freezing and that they had better get something to cover me. They replied that as soon as Tricia's took off, a second Life Flight would land for me.

What? Life Flight for me? Was I hurt worse than I realized? Did this mean that both boys were already dead, and there was no need for them to be flown to the medical center?

I really didn't have time to think about it: with a storm of air and sound, the helicopter took off, and moments later a second one landed. I was put on a gurney, covered with warm sheets and a blanket, and stowed in the back. With the high-pitched scream of jet turbines, we took off and began our eight-minute flight to the Houston Medical Center, part of perhaps the finest network of hospitals in the country. If anyone could keep my family alive, the medical staff there could.

MINUTE 30—FLASHBACK

As we flew, I caught occasional glimpses of freeways and buildings through the copilot's floor windows. My mind jumped back six months to my only other helicopter ride. The boys and I were in Colorado, on an adventure to celebrate my fifty-fifth birthday. We spent one day mountain biking and another racing along challenging trails on four-wheel ATVs. But my favorite part of the trip was the two days of intense white-water rafting on the Arkansas River as it snaked through the Royal Gorge. While on the river, we saw a sleek red helicopter crest the gorge 1,100 feet above us, roll into a steep dive, and pull up just before hitting the river. It rocketed fifty feet over us, blasting us with downdraft. All six of us guys in the raft went wild.

The next day we took the ride.

It was like a roller coaster without tracks. Incredible! The boys and I enjoyed it so much that we did it again two days later before coming home; it was one of the most wonderful memories of my life. But as I looked out at the lights of the hospital landing pad, remembering that fantastic trip, I felt as though I were watching the home videos of some other person; there was just no connection. I was numb.

MINUTE 40—IN THE TRAUMA UNIT

It took only a moment for the trauma team to whisk me inside, where I was surrounded by doctors and nurses—none of whom would tell me anything about my family. The next thing I knew, my mom and dad were there. Someone from the hospital administration arrived, and when I asked her about my wife and sons, she told me not to worry: my son Bart was being transferred by ambulance and would arrive shortly. He would be treated in this same room, just a few feet from me. That told me everything. They were only working on two of us.

I turned to my parents. "Mom, I think there's a good chance that Tricia and Kevin are dead." Turning to the woman from administration, I asked, "Isn't that so?" She looked at me for a long moment, nodded her head, and said that it was.

Bart was wheeled into the room a few moments later. I learned that he had rushed into the dark house and, in an apparent scuffle with the shooter, had been shot in the left arm. He was in shock, reacting to the horror of everything. The trauma team scurried around, cleaning wounds and applying temporary casts, since both of us had broken arms. The bullet had entered my right shoulder and traveled through the arm muscle, striking midhumerus and shattering the bone. Bart's upper left arm was broken where the bullet had hit. Amid the organized chaos, things began to sink in; God was allowing the truth to come a little at a time.

I felt God's presence and comfort. On the one hand I was beginning to absorb how radically things had changed, while on the other I had a calm assurance that I was not alone and that God would knit whatever happened into his plans for good. Scriptures of comfort came to mind. It was as if God gave me a shot of emotional Novocain. Even though I was becoming more aware of the extent of the tragedy, I trusted God.

Before I knew it, I was being wheeled out of the trauma center and into a corridor. As we passed through the big emergency room doors, I was met by forty or fifty friends. Rolling through a canyon of loved ones, I was touched by the grief and worry in their eyes, and began to comfort them. I can't explain it; the words just came out. My response was unexpected and somewhat out of character.

Later that night, after the nurses had gone, I was finally alone with my thoughts. I lay there trying to wrap my mind around it all—and wasn't doing a very good job. Piece by piece the reality settled onto my soul.

MINUTE 180—REALITY AND CHOICES

My wife, my lover, my best friend, the one who knew and loved me better than any other, to whom I had been true for twenty-eight years, was dead. My son Kevin, with his incredible Christian faith, his crazy, fun-loving personality, and his passion for sports and the outdoors, would never graduate from college, marry, or give us grandchildren. Bart was down the hall suffering a grief and shock that seemed even more intense than what I was feeling. At fifty-five, I would be facing the last third of my life without most of my family.

For years I have told people that faith is not a feeling

but a conscious act of will. You have to choose to trust and believe, especially when circumstances and your feelings are screaming that you can't trust God. The Bible says that God can take everything and work it for good for those who love him and are called to his service; well, Tricia and Kevin loved him, and so did I. We were all called to his service, but how could these murders possibly be worked for good? I could imagine no such scenario. And if that verse of the Bible was untrustworthy, what other verses might not apply when I needed them? I might as well throw it all away.

So here I was, in the middle of a horrific situation in which I had to choose to either go with my feelings and slip into bitterness and despair, or follow my own advice and stand on God's promises even when they don't make sense. I wrestled with this for a long time because I knew that I could go either way—and that the consequences could be serious.

Finally, I chose to stand on the promises of God. It was one of the most important decisions I've ever made.

When I resolved to trust God, I felt a peace come over me that had nothing to do with the morphine drip. Then the next thought popped unexpectedly into my mind: *What about the shooter?*

I realized that God was offering me the ability to forgive, if I wanted to take advantage of it. Did I really want to forgive this guy? I know the Bible says we are to forgive those who hurt us. I know God tells us that vengeance is his, if he chooses to dispense it. I have even heard secular health professionals say that forgiveness is the most important thing people can do to heal themselves. But did I really want to forgive, even if God was offering a supernatural ability to do so?

In an instant the answer sprang full-grown into my mind. My heart told me that I wanted whoever was responsible to come to Christ and repent for this awful act. At that moment I felt myself completely forgiving him. This forgiveness astounded me, because earlier I had experienced feelings of incredible sadness and intense anger—even the desire to kill the person responsible with my own hands. Little did I realize just how important my decision to forgive would be in the coming months. It would change everything.

I have had a hundred people tell me that they think I'm nuts—that I should hate the shooter and cry out for vengeance. Perhaps I am crazy, but I believe that in those early moments God worked supernaturally, allowing me to forgive completely and immediately because he had plans for me, and those plans required that I settle the forgiveness problem once and for all.

For the next two days, as Bart and I waited in our rooms for surgery, we had a nearly unprecedented number of visitors. People were always lined up in the halls waiting to see us; they came and went day and night. In fact, the crowding was so severe that the hospital converted a double room on our floor into a hospitality suite stocked with fruit baskets, cookies, coffee, soft drinks, sofas, and chairs. The hospital showed a lot of class, but I think crowd control was also an important factor.

The next day I had my first visit from Detective Marshall Slot and his partner Billy Baugh from the Sugar Land Police Department. They questioned me extensively about what had happened, and I cooperated, telling them I would do everything I could to help them find out who was responsible for this murderous attack.

The detectives returned a day later to tell me they had learned that Bart was not about to graduate from college after all. In fact, he was not even enrolled in school. I was shocked at the news and horrified at the realization that, if this was true, this knowledge coupled with some mistakes Bart had made years earlier might distract the police from searching for the real killer and lead them to look at Bart as a possible suspect. Marshall told me that they were looking at every possibility, which confirmed my fears.

After they left I fumbled my way into a wheelchair and rolled down to Bart's room, where I found him asleep, as he seemed to be whenever I came to visit. It was as if he had crawled into a hole, trying to escape this nightmare. I asked his girlfriend (who had camped out at the hospital since the first morning) for a few minutes alone with my son.

"Bart, what were you thinking? You weren't even in school? How could you lie to us about graduation?"

Bart seemed to forcibly pull himself out of some private hell as he sat up in his bed. The curtains were closed, and the room was dark. Gloom pervaded the atmosphere, with those areas just outside the edge of my vision in deepest shadow. At the time the thought did little more than register in my subconscious, but I would later recall this oppressive darkness and do much thinking about it. For now, my thoughts were focused on Bart. A momentary flicker of strange emotions danced in his eyes; he seemed to career between grief, shame, regret, and fear.

"Dad, I'm so sorry! I didn't want to tell you because I knew how much you and Mom were looking forward to my graduation. I just figured I could work it out and take the classes next semester, and nobody would know."

"Nobody would know!" I was furious. "How would we not know? How would they let you graduate? How did you get into this mess in the first place?"

"Things were crazy at work all summer. Some guys quit, everybody was working long hours, and with school starting, I just didn't have enough time. I'm so sorry! I decided to help at work and make up school in the spring."

"Do you have any idea what you've done? Thanks to this 'little' lie about graduation, the police think you're a suspect! In fact, right now you seem to be their only suspect. You weren't in school, you told everyone you were graduating, and they think you arranged to have us killed to cover it up. Can you see how stupid that was? Your lie has done the impossible—It has made Tricia's and Kevin's deaths even worse because now the police think you were involved! Do you have any idea how bad this is?"

Years ago, on a bike ride, I saw a hawk fly right over me, so close I could almost touch it. Clutched within its talons was a field mouse, still alive. I saw the bird swoop up to its nest, bringing breakfast to her young; it would be impossible to forget the look of resignation and terror in the mouse's eyes as he passed over me. For a moment I saw the same look in Bart's eyes, but it was gone almost instantly, replaced with resolve.

"Dad, that's nuts! I didn't have anything to do with the shootings! I'm sorry about the lie, it just happened. I didn't mean to lie to you and Mom—I was just afraid of what you would say, and I didn't want to disappoint you. This will be okay."

"I don't know. I'm so mad now, I could spit! I've told you before: you cannot ever allow yourself to start lying again! Look at the consequences of this one! If you hadn't told the lie about graduation, they would be looking elsewhere and might find the real killer before the trail gets cold. Now they're wasting time on you, and who knows how long they'll keep at it!"

After a while I calmed down, and I told him I loved him and that the police would soon realize nothing tied him to the shootings. I went back to my room, still angry, disappointed, and depressed. What would happen next?

As the days passed, two things happened: First, the investigation centered more and more on Bart as the mastermind of a plot to kill the rest of the family, assuming that his motives were greed and to cover up failures at school. Second, I came to realize that perhaps my life had been spared for a reason. God must have something important for me to do, because I could see no logical explanation for my still being alive. The bullet hit me well away from my right lung, and nearly six inches from my heart. The gunman couldn't have been that bad a shot. Not at that close range.

It occurred to me that perhaps my purpose was to be God's agent of guidance and instruction for Bart. If he was innocent,

I would be the anchor he relied on as he weathered the storms of suspicion; I wouldn't let him go through that horror alone. If he was guilty, I would be in a unique position to model God's unconditional forgiveness and love. I might be the person God would use to soften Bart's heart. And since I already had forgiven whoever was responsible, if Bart was guilty, he would be covered in a pure forgiveness, granted before I ever thought it might apply to my son. Either way, until I knew more, I would be nonjudgmental and supportive. While I couldn't gloss over anything or minimize the consequences of any wrongs Bart might have committed, I still needed to show him that God forgives and that there is always hope.

Maybe I'm crazy. But I took comfort in knowing that I was doing what God wanted me to do. I like reading that line in the Bible about the wisdom of God being foolishness to man. Maybe a nut was exactly whom God intended to use.

Chapter 2

DUST TO DUST

DECEMBER 13, 2003

Bart and I were scheduled for back-to-back surgeries on Saturday morning. I joked with the nurses that my biggest concern was that they used the correct rods in the correct arms: if you held the X-rays from our respective wounds next to each other, they looked like mirror images. Bart's left arm was affected, and my right; neither had exit wounds since both bullets had shattered upon impact and the pieces were scattered among the bone fragments. Our surgeon, Dr. Jeffrey Tucker, decided to insert a permanent titanium rod through the soft marrow of the humerus bone, and over time the fragments would fuse together around it. The rod would be attached by

15

2021670.2

screws to the shoulder and the elbow, giving structural integrity to the arm until the healing was complete in about three months. Removing the dozen bullet fragments would have damaged the surrounding muscle tissue and created lots of scarring, so he left them in place. We became real bionic men.

DECEMBER 14—WELCOME HOME

Bart and I went home Sunday morning. As my brother Keith drove us into the neighborhood, we were met with an amazing sight: the trees in the esplanade and in most of the yards were wrapped with big yellow ribbons. They were everywhere. Tears rushed to my eyes, and I felt comforted but also apprehensive about how I would react when we got home. It felt surreal to consider walking up to the house in which we had lived for twenty years and passing through the front door where Tricia and Kevin had fallen. I wasn't sure I could do it. Yet once again I had become emotionally numb and was only able to catalog the data, like some reconnaissance cyborg. I was a man detached, watching the movie of someone else's life.

I made it past the entryway without trouble, only to be surprised that the house looked just as it had when we went to dinner four days and a lifetime ago. How amazing that it should be the same when everything else had changed.

I later learned that after the police completed their investigation, they turned the house over to an army of friends who decided they would not let us come home to bloodstained carpets. With the help of my insurance agent and donations from friends, they replaced the downstairs carpeting. Countless Christmas decorations had to be moved, including a fully decorated, eight-foot tree. A crew of women took about a hundred Polaroid pictures of everything so that when the new carpet was installed, they could put everything back just as it had been. Knowing how long it had taken us to decorate in the first place, I was amazed that they were able to do it all in just one day!

Friends continued to drop by for weeks, and I enjoyed seeing everyone except the television crews that sometimes camped out in the cul-de-sac. Food was everywhere, with more arriving all the time. My challenge was to find a place in the fridge for everything. For years I had attended a weekly Bible study with a group of guys; we called ourselves the FAT men (Faithful, Available, and Teachable), and that afternoon, after I awoke from a much-needed nap, six of the FAT men came by. They told me they were going to make sure that I was not alone: every night for a few weeks, one of them would sleep on my couch. So with all the food and people, Bart and I were going to be well supported.

The first night was strange. Besides Bart, half a dozen friends and family were there, and every light in the house was on. Suddenly I had a panic attack, terrified that the killer was outside, lurking in the dark shadows, watching us and waiting to finish what he had started. After all, the investigation had barely begun, and we had no clue as to the motive behind the shootings. The police didn't think we had interrupted a burglary (what I had originally assumed) because none of the electronics, jewelry, or other valuables had been taken. I had no enemies that I knew of. I had been in the construction business for thirty years, and had the respect of vendors, clients, and even friendly competitors. I had no idea why this had happened. After suggesting that we close the curtains and avoid walking through any rooms that had unobstructed views to the outside, I tried to turn on the burglar alarm but was told that the police had disabled it— not because of any malfunction or matter of procedure but as the result of one officer's curiosity.

It turns out that around three o'clock on the night of the shootings, as the crime scene crews were finishing their work, detectives were about to come downstairs when one of them stopped next to a panic button that I had installed when the house was built. I figured that if we ever had an intruder, we'd need to trip the alarm instantly. I had also installed one downstairs, in the master bedroom. The detectives had noticed it all evening but had no idea what it was for, and one of them finally gave in to curiosity and pushed the button. The alarm went off, shrieking at one hundred decibels, waking up the neighbors and starting every dog in the neighborhood barking. Since the police didn't have the code to turn it off, they eventually located the horn and cut the wires—thus restoring peace but leaving us without a functioning alarm.

When I realized that we couldn't turn it on, I felt horribly exposed. The police had told me to call if I ever became worried, so I asked them to send over an officer while I reconnected the siren. The policeman told me that they had boosted the patrols past our house, and the next day the Sugar Land

Police Department responded to local concern by increasing their presence to the point of keeping a unit parked in the cul-de-sac around the clock for nearly two weeks. It helped everyone in our neighborhood to feel safer.

THE FUNERAL

On Monday evening a visitation was scheduled at the funeral home. Friends had told me that I didn't need to attend, and since I wasn't sure I was emotionally ready to be out in public with so many people, I had planned to spend a quiet evening at home.

But after a nap that afternoon, I was doing better and felt an obligation to attend. We had seen a few of the news reports on television, and (as attested by the yellow ribbons everywhere) the whole community was grieving. I decided to go so everyone would know that we were all right. Getting into a suit was tricky, since I no longer had the use of my dominant arm, but somehow I got a tie on and fixed my collar. Bart and I ended up staying at the funeral home for ninety minutes, and when we left, about two hundred people were still there. I had a rough time falling asleep that night, realizing that the funeral would be the next morning.

The day dawned absolutely beautifully: bright, clear, and cool. It was the kind of day on which Tricia would have persuaded me to join her on a long walk. But we would share no more of those. I had seen the last of her playful skipping or trying to trip me as she pointed out a bird. There would be no more sudden hand squeezes or hugs. For a moment the aching hole in my heart made me wish that the gunman had finished the job.

Promptly at nine o'clock, the car from the funeral home arrived to take us to Sugar Creek Baptist, which had been our church home for six years before our move to nondenominational River Pointe Community Church. The services couldn't be held at River Pointe because its facilities weren't large enough for the expected crowd. Sugar Creek, however, fit the needs well: the largest church in the Sugar Land area, it seated three thousand and had the internal television and audio equipment needed to provide a media feed for all the Houston news channels, which would broadcast the service live. The seating capacity was important since estimates predicted a crowd of nearly two thousand people. Family friend and high-profile defense lawyer Dan Cogdell commented that he had been to funerals for former governors with fewer attendees.

A large group of family members gathered in the waiting area behind the stage. We visited, drinking coffee and orange juice. I wandered around and couldn't help but remember the last time I had been in that huge room.

It was the night Kevin graduated from high school, and the commencement had been held in the church. Before the ceremony, all the graduating seniors had gathered back there, and Tricia and I snuck in to get some pictures of the kids. Everyone was in high spirits, and Kevin joked that we needed to watch him as he stepped forward to get his diploma. Knowing Kevin's penchant for practical jokes, I reminded him that he still hadn't graduated and wasn't home free yet. He laughed and told us not to worry—just watch. So when the ceremony reached the point where students were called up to receive their diplomas, we held our breaths, wondering what was coming. One by one his friends came forward, some with special-colored ropes hanging over their graduation gowns to signify their inclusion in the honor society or other academic accolades. Although Kevin had been his junior class president and was a leader in the school, he was ranked in the middle of his class scholastically, so he hadn't received any such honor cords. But when his name was called, he stepped forward, grinning, with a six-foot white electrical extension cord draped over his shoulders. The superintendent and high school principal burst into laughter and just shook their heads. Typical Kevin.

And now we were in the same room, getting ready to tell him a final good-bye.

When the time came, the family was led into the foyer, and Tricia's younger brother (and my business partner for years) suggested that Bart and I peek through one of the side doors at the crowd that was assembling; he felt we needed to be prepared for the numbers. I was surprised to see so many people.

We reached the main aisle and began the long walk down to the front. Two closed caskets sat there, blanketed in roses, and flower arrangements and sprays covered the stage. Months later I would learn that the police had hidden microphones among the flowers to record anything that might be said, in case someone involved in the shootings made a quiet statement to the deceased. We took our seats and the service began.

From the first day in the hospital, when my pastor and

best friend, Matt Barnhill, talked to me about my wishes for the service, I had told him that I would leave the details up to him; so I wasn't sure exactly how the service would go. About all I knew was that Kevin's and Tricia's friends had put together two videos and that Matt would lead the main part of the service. My only direct instructions to him were that the service should be a celebration, because I knew that Tricia and Kevin were in heaven. And I had requested that, if possible, Aaron Ivey be the featured vocalist. Tricia and I had known Aaron for several years and were impressed with his talent and character. He was the lead singer for Spur 58, a local Christian rock band that Kevin loved. Two years earlier, Kevin had brought the band to our family lake house for four days of writing music and horsing around in the water. Aaron had since moved to Nashville with his young wife to pursue a recording career, but thanks to some friends who picked up the tab, he was able to fly in for the service. So other than knowing that he was going to sing my favorite traditional hymn, "A Mighty Fortress Is Our God," and Tricia's favorite contemporary Christian song, "The Midnight Cry," I didn't know what to expect.

The service was more beautiful than I could have imagined: full of love, bittersweet humor and laughter, and remembrances of good times. Tricia's Ladies' Bible Study leader, Mary Willis, spoke of her, reminding us of her impish humor and infectious joy. Kevin's oldest friend, Cale Donaldson, and Kevin's best friend, Brittany Barnhill (Matt's daughter, and the girl Tricia and I had secretly hoped would become Kevin's wife), both spoke of him. When they were through and Aaron had finished singing, Matt delivered a beautiful message, barely keeping his composure. He spoke of how alike Tricia and Kevin had been in many ways, with their passion for serving others, their tender hearts, and especially their clever wit and zest for life. He shared how Tricia was the consummate hostess, not because of her endless supply of themed decorations and clever food preparations—although those were as much a part of her as her laughter—but because it was all done to honor her guests. She didn't have a prideful or mean-spirited bone in her body and was concerned only with making her guests feel special and at home, never with showing off. As Matt said, whenever you did something with Tricia, it involved food and fun.

Matt then introduced the music and video presentations put together by Tricia's and Kevin's friends. They brought back so many memories: Tricia the kindergarten teacher on the school playground in her flannel pajamas for "Wear Pajamas to School Day"; Kevin on one of his World Changers mission trips to repair homes for poverty-stricken families in the Arkansas hills; Tricia astride her horse, the beloved Millie Diamond; head coach Kevin as he led the junior class girls to victory over the seniors in the Powder Puff Football Classic; Tricia and me in Austin, enjoying a surprise minivacation that Bart had bought for us at a charity auction; and many, many more, all precious.

The service closed with an open-mike opportunity for anyone who wanted to speak. Kevin's friend John Flores told a story that typified Kevin's craziness: Both boys were freshmen at Texas A&M when John borrowed a pair of Kevin's dress slacks. A week later, Kevin came to pick them up, and when John opened his apartment door, there stood Kevin, in starched polo shirt, socks, dress shoes, and . . . a pair of brightly colored boxer shorts. He had walked all the way across campus in his underwear!

THE LONG DRIVE

The motorcade to the graveside was 250 cars long and must have wreaked havoc on local traffic as it wound through town to the cemetery. Following a short service and the two interments, a large crowd of family and friends stopped at Tricia's mom's home for lunch. Again I had entered that surrealistic zone where I could visit with everyone but felt detached and numb. At one point I even walked upstairs and stood in Tricia's old bedroom, looking at pictures of her taken nearly thirty-five years earlier, when I first met her. How young we had both been! I thought about the five years we had dated and all the events that had been held in that house, including our wedding reception. I thought about the picture we had taken of three-year-old Kevin, snuggled up with his beloved "Papa" (Tricia's late father, Bill) as they both slept away a Thanksgiving afternoon in Bill's recliner. I felt a huge wave of sadness, loss, and envy as I suddenly had a vision of all three, once again together, snuggled up in the lap of our heavenly Father. I just stood there in her room, wishing I knew what to do next.

If I could have looked into the future and seen the storm clouds that were even then beginning to form, I might have savored that time of solitude; but as it was, all I felt was a profound sense of separation.

The morning after the funeral, I was restless, needing to do something, so I went to work and prepared the company paychecks. I knew that if I stood still, I would start remembering everything, and it was much easier to stay busy and keep those hounds at bay. Bart must have been feeling the same, because he came to work with me. Between the two of us, I got the checks cut. From that point on I would go to work almost every day, which I was able to justify because as comptroller, I had a lot of work to get done before the closing of the fiscal year.

THE FIRST CHRISTMAS

Christmas was little more than a week away, and I hadn't done much gift buying. As in many homes, my wife would do most of our Christmas shopping, and I would go at the last minute. I knew that Tricia had purchased many things for the boys and for both of our families, but I was clueless as to what they were or where she had hidden them. One night I turned the house upside down looking for presents. The hunt forced me to search through many things loaded with powerful memories. For example, I knew that she often hid things in her closet and her bedroom drawers, but when I opened the first drawer and started looking through her nightgowns, my emotions screamed in panic. It would be months before I could go back through some of the drawers.

I decided to wrap what gifts I could find and give the rest

as they turned up. But I still had to get through Christmas.

Our tradition was to spend Christmas Eve with my family, exchanging gifts with my mom and dad, brothers, sister, in-laws, nephews and nieces, aunts and uncles, cousins, and various quasi family. As all our kids grew up, we began giving white elephant gifts. The goal was to find something that held some value (though inexpensive) but which was in such hideously bad taste that you would not want it inside your house, or was so esoteric that it would be useless to the average person. Sometimes we would open a gift and have no idea what its function was.

A great deal of pride went along with bringing the worst gift. Everyone would bring these odd treasures, all camouflaged in bright Christmas wrappings, and if you didn't know better, you'd think the pile represented some serious Christmas booty. We would begin by picking numbers out of a hat, and when your number came up, you would choose a gift, either from the pile of those yet unopened or, if someone had previously opened something that might conceivably be useful to you or that matched your quirks, you could pounce on it and claim it for yourself. The person losing his or her treasure would then use your number to pick something else.

Even in the shadow of tragedy it was lots of fun, with whoops of hilarity as gift after gift was revealed, and I enjoyed the evening immensely. Everyone was aware of the two empty chairs, but it was comforting to be laughing with loved ones. After eating, we all went to what my mom calls "High Church" at the beautiful old St. Paul's Methodist, where my parents are members. The service was majestic and moving, and with a huge choir and massive pipe organ, the music was spectacular—not at all like the amplified contemporary Christian music and casual attire I was used to at River Pointe. After church, Bart, his girlfriend, and I said our good-byes to everyone, and we went together to her dad's home to spend the night.

I was grateful to them for including me in their family's Christmas. I'm not sure I could have spent Christmas in my house, and they made me feel wonderfully welcome. I actually slept well and awoke Christmas morning to the aroma of a delicious breakfast. We opened gifts, relaxed for a while, and then drove to her uncle's home for a huge lunch and a round of their version of the white elephant gift exchange; although I must say, their gag gifts were a lot nicer and more practical than the crazy things my family came up with. I left in the late afternoon, thankful that I had been so blessed. I had gotten through my first two weeks and holiday without Tricia and Kevin. Next up, New Year's.

Chapter 3

NEW YEAR'S EVE: LOOKING FORWARD, LOOKING BACK

New Year's Eve used to come in three categories: (1) loud, exciting ones in crowded, public places; (2) small, quiet parties with close friends; and (3) private, intimate dinners with Tricia.

On December 31, 2003, I added a fourth category: eating a frozen dinner and watching *Twilight Zone* reruns by myself. Appropriate, I guess, since I felt like I was living in one of Rod Serling's scripts.

Once I got past that first night out of the hospital, things settled into a strange routine. I would hear the front door close as my FAT-man friend who had been sleeping on the sofa left for the salt mines. Bart and I would get up and eat breakfast, and I would go to work. Sometimes Bart would accompany me, and other days he would run errands. As the afternoon drew to a close, we would trickle back in and eat something from the vast array of food left by friends. Then Bart and I would sit down and take turns reading pages and discussing that day's chapter of Rick Warren's *The Purpose-Driven Life.* Sometimes my FAT-man friend would get there in time to join in the reading, and then we would talk, watch television, or do things individually until it was time to clean our wounds before going to bed.

Bart and I spent a lot of time together, and I began what would be a seven-month discipleship of my son. Besides reading *The Purpose-Driven Life,* we read John Ortberg's *If You Want to Walk on Water, You've Got to Get Out of the Boat,* and others. We held long, frank, and in-depth discussions on grace, forgiveness, and healing, exploring together. In those first days, when the police became convinced that Bart was involved in the shooting, I realized that he (who had never been as strong in his faith as the rest of us) was going to need spiritual guidance, whether the police were right or wrong. If he was innocent, he was going to need to grow in his faith to handle the pressures of suspicion and perhaps even a trial; if he was guilty, he needed to truly believe that repentance brings God's forgiveness. Having intellectual knowledge of the gospel of forgiveness is one thing, but it's entirely different to know it in your heart and accept it to the point that you can forgive yourself, trusting that nothing is beyond God's love for us.

Either way, it would be easier for Bart to understand God's love if he saw it acted out in the flesh, and this was my opportunity.

Within a week of returning home, Bart and I experienced a strange turn of events. The police asked if we would take a polygraph test, and when we both agreed, it was scheduled for the Monday before Christmas. But as I was leaving for the police station, Detective Slot called to cancel it, telling me that the Department of Public Safety officer who was to administer the tests had decided to take off early for Christmas. Marshall said it would be rescheduled after New Year's, but it never was.

Looking back over the last four years, I see God's hand all over this. In the days before Christmas, I ranked the possibility of Bart's involvement in the murders at perhaps 5 percent. Even then I didn't believe he had anything to do with the shootings; I reasoned that he might have gotten into trouble with a bad crowd and could have arranged for us to be out of the house for a payoff burglary that went bad. I had expected the polygraph test to prove our innocence, so I was disappointed that it didn't happen on schedule. However, hindsight has shown me that God did not want the investigation to be over so soon. I think he wanted Bart to have those seven months of mentoring. By the time he was arrested in 2005, he had done the hard introspection and was ready for the second half of my work, which was to display true forgiveness in spite of everything. But as yet we knew nothing of what was coming.

One surprise brought me great joy during those first two weeks. Bart explained that the shootings had caused him to realize how short life was, and that he was going to propose to his girlfriend of five years when they went to their annual New Year's Eve party in Austin. This was wonderful news. Tricia and I loved her and for a long time had wanted to see them married. He spent a week shopping for a diamond ring, and just after Christmas he chose one. The surprise almost fell apart, however, because she was adamant about skipping the Austin party and staying home with me so I wouldn't be lonely. It was all I could do to convince her that I wanted to be alone, to think.

Two days before New Year's Eve, Bart and I took down all the Christmas decorations and hauled the tree out to be picked up by the recycling crew. Normally the decorations would have been left up until after New Year's, but I was ready to put it all away. So many raw memories were associated with them.

Tricia had always decorated the fireplace mantel, draping it with freshly cut evergreen branches. Intertwined with the greenery were six or seven large nutcrackers, candlesticks of varying sizes, huge pinecones, and some tastefully placed items selected from her huge trove of Christmas decorations. Every year she would fiddle with it until it was time to take it all down—moving a candlestick or a nutcracker a half inch this way or that, clipping a small branch here and there, trying to get it perfect. Sometimes she would take it all down and start over, using completely different nutcrackers or going back to the tree lot to beg for more branches. You could almost keep track of the days by noting the little modifications. This year the process had been only a week and a half old when she died. It always looked perfect to me, but knowing that she would never make another adjustment made me sad. It was the first thing I took down.

The next thing boxed up was a ceramic village of small-town America. Years ago it had become a tradition for Kevin to set up this turn-of-the-century community on the sofa-back table, and although he professed to being tired of doing it, he always took great pride in arranging the many buildings and figures. The final step was to sprinkle the fake snow, and he did it a pinch at a time so it would be just right. One year I bumped the table, knocking a good bit of snow and the church onto the floor. He teased me that if the oxen in Bethlehem had been that clumsy, they would have knocked over the manger, and then he spent twenty minutes repairing the damage. We called it Kevin Corners, and I was acutely aware of every little piece as I put them away. I haven't touched any of it since.

The tree was the last to go, and that was traditionally in my purview, since I was as much a perfectionist about the lights being balanced as Tricia was about the mantel and Kevin his village. After the lights were placed to my liking, I loosely braided three ribbons, draping them and adding big bows here and there. If Bart were in town, he would join us and hang the ornaments once I finished with the lights and ribbons. My cycling buddies would have given me a lot of flack about my artistic endeavors if they had known, because the tree always came out looking like something from a Martha Stewart magazine.

They say that of all the senses, smell carries the most intense memories. Perhaps that was why the decorations bothered me so. Every time I went into the living room, I was assaulted by pleasant fragrances carrying painful memories of wonderful things that were gone forever. After four years, I still have not put up another Christmas tree.

So New Year's Eve found me alone, in a house back to "normal" and empty of Christmas trappings. I had spent much of the afternoon thinking and processing the many ways my life had changed, and although profoundly aware of my situation, I felt at peace. I knew that the approaching year would be difficult, but with a coming wedding and (hopefully) the police redirecting their focus away from Bart, I could get through it. By the time it got dark, I was ready to eat and bid a relaxing adieu to the old year with the screen works of Rod Serling, hoping that the New Year would bring peace and healing to my grieving heart.

Around a quarter to twelve, I decided to go for a walk. The winter night was mild, with a light fog. I was surprised at how empty the neighborhood was. Though I had expected to see cars parked along the street for parties, I didn't see a single one. There was no traffic. I was walking through the foggy world alone, on more than one level. Midnight came and went, and I heard a car horn celebrate far away. Someone set off firecrackers just within hearing, but other than that, I was a solitary traveler.

Back home, I turned off the lights and sat on the stairs for a long time, praying. Then I went to sleep wondering what the New Year would bring. As it turned out, 2004 would bring even more heartaches and radical changes. I would realize that, like King David of old, I had been living for years with a plotting, troubled son like Absalom. The roller coaster was just beginning its run.

Chapter 4

STORM CLOUDS OF SUSPICION

Within hours of the shootings, clouds of suspicion gathered around Bart. While the police considered him a suspect from the start, no one who knew him believed it. And although the detectives learned some things very early on that kept them focused on Bart, they didn't share any of that with me. I'm sure that if we had known what they knew, our subsequent actions would have been different. I now know that all the support Bart received from his loved ones had been bought with lies.

But at this stage we were still in the dark and torn between believing Bart and believing the police. Our conflict was heightened because we were all strong supporters of law enforcement. I was a life member of the Houston 100 Club, which helps support the families of police officers who lose their lives in the line of duty, and my father had served on several Houston grand juries. We were a law-and-order family caught in a nightmare.

Should we believe the police and their vague and un- proven claims? Should we believe Bart and reject the officers' warnings simply because Bart claimed they were false? Too little information was available for a rational person to know whom to believe. Trying to keep an open mind to both possi- bilities, my position was clear to everyone: I would cooperate with the police in every way, but I wouldn't abandon my son simply because they wanted me to. Neither would I blindly proclaim his innocence, because I knew they might be right; but until they showed me some proof to support their claims, I was not going to turn my back on the last surviving member of my family.

OTHER POSSIBILITIES

Was Bart the only suspect? On the night of the shootings, a man took his own life as the police closed in on him. Shortly before he shot himself, he placed a cell phone call to his girl- friend, telling her that he had killed someone, that the police were near, and that he wasn't going back to prison. Officers found his body, still clad in a ski mask and gloves, in an apart- ment storage closet on Corporate Drive. Corporate Drive is less than two miles from my home. The incident was reported on television that evening and in the next morning's paper.

In the weeks and months that followed, I repeatedly asked what the police had learned about that suicide, but I never got a direct answer. They would only say that nothing indicated that the man was involved in the incident at our house. When I pressed for details, I got nowhere. I asked what time the suicide had occurred, because if it was before we were attacked, he would have been dead and obviously not a suspect; but they either didn't know or wouldn't tell me. I know of at least one other Corporate Drive in the Houston area, and it's miles away. Knowing which cell phone tower received the signal when he placed the call would confirm his location; I don't know whether they checked on that. For all we knew, the shooter could have placed the call as he left our neighborhood just minutes before taking his own life.

And what about the strange events surrounding a girl who had wanted to date Kevin, and her reportedly jealous and violent boyfriend? The night before the shooting, Tricia was roused from bed around eleven o'clock by an engine idling in front of our house. She recognized the truck as one owned by a girl who knew Kevin, and she saw Kevin get out of the vehicle and walk to our back door as the girl drove off. Always concerned about what was going on in the boys' lives, she spoke with Kevin before coming back to bed, where she told me of their conversation. Kevin explained that the girl had called his cell phone upset and wanting to talk, so he spoke with her in the truck for about twenty minutes. The girl broke down, telling Kevin that she didn't know what to do: she had liked Kevin for a long time. She was thinking about breaking up with her boyfriend, hoping that she could then start dating Kevin instead. He told her that while he valued her friendship, he wasn't going to start dating her.

The next night Kevin was dead.

On the night of the shooting, word spread like wildfire among Kevin's friends. Two of them arrived within twenty minutes, and as they approached the stop sign five houses from our home, they were surprised to see the girl already standing there. She asked them for a ride because she didn't have her truck with her. She rode with them to the hospital, and afterward they took her home. She didn't live in our neighborhood, and to this day, I don't know how she got there so quickly without transportation. Had the police questioned her?

Although I repeatedly requested that these two people be investigated to determine where they had been that night, the extent of the inquiry was a visit with the girl weeks later, and the official answer was simply, "Nothing there." To the best of my knowledge, the three friends who found her without transportation near the scene of the crime were never questioned about this.

Both of these leads seemed to deserve timely and thorough investigation, but as far as I could tell, they never got it. I felt that they were just as worthy of consideration as the possibility that Bart was involved, but the police never gave me any indication that these leads received anything more than a cursory look. If they had truly investigated both possibilities and had shared with me why these theories were dead ends, I would have been satisfied; however, I got the impression every time I pursued the issue that I was being stonewalled.

CURIOUS REASONING

Besides all but ignoring these leads, to those of us on the outside, the investigators seemed to display lapses in reasoning. For example, the police are still holding as evidence the belt and boots I wore on the night of the shooting because "they might produce evidence at some time in the future when diagnostic procedures get better." Using that logic, no evidence in any case would ever be released. (The trial has been over for more than a year now.) It was weeks before they returned my eyeglasses, and then only because I told them that they were my only pair of prescription lenses. How my items of clothing could provide evidence is beyond me, since they never entered the house and no one else ever touched them. Although the police immediately confiscated two computers we had in our home and two laptops from Bart's house, keeping them for months, they never took Bart's main desktop computer to see what was on it. In fact, they never even conducted a detailed search of his home, nor did they try opening a safe that he kept there. They did conduct detailed interviews with Bart's many fellow workers and acquaintances, but they only interviewed two of Kevin's friends. Months later, when Bart fled the country for a period of time, his vehicle sat unused for a week before detectives came to look through it.

My question about the postponed lie detector test was never answered. As time passed I often wondered why this test was never rescheduled. If it had been given, many things might have come to light years sooner. Everything would have been different.

These things concerned me greatly, so as a cautionary move in January 2004, we retained family friend and defense attorney Dan Cogdell to represent Bart in case something came of all the allegations. Dan contacted two nationally known homicide detectives, both of whom he had known before they retired. One had been the dean of homicide from the Houston Police Department, and the other had held a similar position within the Texas Rangers. Both offered to help our Sugar Land Police Department, but both were told by the SLPD that they were not needed.

I feared that our young police department, without much experience in conducting murder investigations, was operating beyond its capacity. They seemed to be pursuing an unlikely suspect while ignoring other possible leads. Sugar Land had recently and explosively grown from a sleepy little hamlet into the eighth-fastest-growing community in the country. When Tricia and I moved here in 1983, fewer than eight thousand people called Sugar Land home. The city fathers had a Mayberry mentality, and the citizens liked it that way. Over the next twenty years, Houston grew out to meet it. Malls, new subdivisions, and expanded freeway access gave rise to major upscale growth: the 2000 census recorded seventy-five thousand residents. City government experienced growing pains as Sugar Land morphed into a modern metropolitan bedroom community, and the police department was forced to grow and learn new skills. Murder was rare—only a handful in the preceding twenty years. Months would pass before SLPD made any substantive announcement, and a lot of fear was felt in the community. I knew that the local police were facing a real challenge and that they were under a lot of pressure from Sugar Land's affluent citizens to solve this crime.

I was afraid the department was in over its head but refusing outside help because of pride. I had seen this in business a hundred times: a young bull would try to cover his inexperience with bluster, rigidity, and false confidence, fearing to ask for help. It was hard to tell whether we were in a Keystone Kops movie or a Franz Kafka nightmare, but for those outside the investigation, none of it made sense.

As I would later learn, however, my negative impressions were not accurate at all.

BART'S PAST MISTAKES

In truth, the police were on top of the situation. But without input from the authorities, I couldn't know this. In my mind Bart's past brushes with the law were distracting the police from pursuing what I hoped were more realistic leads.

I understood that his prior behavior would raise red flags. Two incidents in particular would've led any prudent person to initially focus on him as a person of interest. Six years earlier, during the summer vacation before his senior year in high school, he and two of his too-smart-for-their-own-good friends figured out a way to bypass their school's burglar alarm by breaking in through the skylights. At first the thrill of doing it was enough; but after a few trips, they decided to take computers as souvenirs—a much more serious crime. Once school resumed, word leaked out and they were caught. Bart was given deferred adjudication with four years of probation. He explained it away as being a prank that got out of hand, but Tricia and I knew that breaking and entering was a lot more serious than the usual schoolboy high jinks. Although Bart said they had planned to return the computers at a later date by leaving them at the school's front door, taking them in the first place was a serious offense.

Bart's arrest for these break-ins was a horrible blow. It occurred the night of his high school's annual open house, which Tricia and I always attended. We heard of the arrest that afternoon and were told that the police would bring Bart back to the school sometime before the open house. Tricia and I arrived early and waited in the school parking lot for over an hour, watching as all the other parents (many of whom we knew) walked past our car. Finally, long after the program had begun, the police car pulled up, and we followed Bart and the officer into the school. Tricia and I met with a counselor, the vice principal, the policeman, and Bart, and then he was taken to jail, which we had not expected. We left in a daze as all the other parents filed past us, going to visit the classes their kids would attend in the morning. Our son would be in jail.

Tricia was in shock. In the coming weeks she slipped into depression, blaming herself. She questioned everything she had done, and when the notice of Bart's arrest appeared in the local newspaper, she felt drowned in shame. She no longer went to her usual grocery store: she'd put on dark glasses and a cap and drive out of the area to shop. If I hadn't forced her to go out once in a while, she would have remained inside, convinced that everyone was whispering about her and Bart.

It took a long time for her to realize that it was Bart and his friends who had made bad choices, and that none of it was her fault. One evening, as we were washing dishes together, she said, "All I ever wanted was to be a good mom!" She looked up at a decorative plate over the sink: the picture showed a little boy and girl holding flowers, and the inscription read, "A Good Mother Makes A Happy Home." Tricia wept.

For Bart's senior year of high school, we transferred him to a private Christian school, where he acquired a new set of friends. He seemed to concentrate on positive activities, and he kept out of trouble. In time we became convinced that Bart had learned his lesson and that the break-ins and theft had merely been a prank that got out of hand, not an indication of a serious character flaw. He made it easy for us to believe this by doing well, and after two years, the judge agreed to terminate Bart's probation early. This meant that Bart would suffer no additional consequences as long as he avoided future trouble. He attended Baylor University in Waco, and except for not getting along with one of his roommates in his second year, he seemed to be making the most of his second chance. We had no idea that he had become a modern-day Absalom, intent on doing us harm.

One of the most prominent figures in Jewish Old Testament history is King David. Long after he slew the giant Goliath, David became Israel's greatest king and an icon personifying the Jewish people's relationship with God. Although he was a man after God's own heart, with many admirable qualities, he also had great weaknesses, and his life (like mine) had its share of tragedy and loss. Perhaps his greatest heartbreak concerned his son Absalom.

Absalom was a gifted young man who killed a brother and tried to kill his father. In the later years of David's reign, his many sons vied for favor in hopes of succession, and Absalom was the most popular of them all. Over a period of years he put into place secret plans to kill his father and gain the inheritance. He led a revolt that almost succeeded in killing David. But a strange thing happened. The father didn't die.

The attempt failed, and Absalom was caught and executed by an overzealous official who knew that Absalom's death was against the father's wishes. When told the news, David wept bitterly, mourning the fate of his murderous son. Many of those around him couldn't understand his tears, pointing out, "Wasn't this the young man who tried to kill you?"

As time passed I began to see just how closely David's and Absalom's lives paralleled Bart's and mine.

Like David with Absalom, Tricia and I didn't know that Bart was bitterly unhappy with his life and was hiding everything from us as his internal pressure grew. It would be three years after the high school break-in before it boiled over into the next incident.

Near the end of Bart's second year at Baylor, Tricia and I were awakened at 1:30 a.m. by a call from the local police to make sure we were safe. They had received a call from the Waco police warning that Bart was on his way to Sugar Land (a four-hour drive) with plans to kill us.

This was the most bizarre thing we had ever heard, and

we immediately discounted it. A policeman came by to check on us, and we visited for quite a while. Naturally, we did what we could to gather information. Tricia and I questioned the officer about what he knew, and we tried to reach Bart on his cell phone, but it was turned off. We talked to his roommate, and he told us there was no problem.

Over the next four days, we pieced together what apparently had happened. According to the police report, a female friend of Bart's roommate had dropped by the apartment. Bart told police that the roommate and his friend had been drinking and had the television volume turned up pretty loud. An argument broke out when Bart asked them several times to leave or turn it down so he could study, which they refused to do. As they argued, a segment came on TV about the Menendez brothers, who were accused of killing their parents. Bart made the offhand remark that they had gone about it all wrong, and when the roommate challenged him, Bart told them how he would do it. The argument escalated, and Bart left angrily. The girl who'd dropped by, and who seemed to have been drinking, called the police with her concern that Bart was actually going to follow through, and this prompted the warning call from the local police to the SLPD.

I didn't know then whether "the friend" was naive, genuinely concerned, merely drunk and misunderstood Bart's statements, or if she just wanted to get back at him for the argument. It never occurred to me that she might have stumbled onto the truth.

When Bart checked his cell phone the next morning and got our messages, he got scared. Fearing that he was going to get into trouble again, he left Waco for two days, and we were frantic with worry because we had no idea where he was. Later, after we had talked to him and the police had investigated, the detective concluded that there was no truth to the charge: it had been simply a misunderstanding brought on by alcohol and tension between roommates.

Looking back, I realize that Bart and his roommate lied about all of it and that the attempt had been real. Thinking of Bart's two-day vanishing act, I am reminded of Proverbs 28:1, which says, "The wicked man flees though no one pursues." While preparing for Bart's trial five years later, I would learn what had really happened, and it still gives me chills. Our Absalom had accidentally shown his hand—but we hadn't recognized the cards.

Perhaps Tricia and I should have seen the signs that something was seriously wrong in Bart's heart, but the shootings came six long years after the incident in high school, and Bart was a master at hiding things from us. The few warning signs were obscured by a forest of success, and we believed that Bart's problems were behind him. I had misjudged things before and no doubt will again. In this case, the consequences of my lack of vision were fatal.

A LUCKY BREAK

Within a few days of the shootings, while Bart and I lay in the hospital, investigators got the kind of lucky break that usually happens only in works of fiction. An old friend of Bart's told the SLPD that two years earlier, Bart had tried to hire him to kill us. In the plan he described, after murdering us, the gunman was to shoot Bart in the left arm to remove suspicion of his involvement. Bart would provide the alarm code and home floor diagram and would arrange to get everyone out of the house and to return at a specified time. The plan had fallen apart, but the details were identical to what had happened in December 2003 and were very similar to what had allegedly been discussed in Waco.

Later the police would learn of yet another attempt, one that nearly succeeded. It took place in December 2000, right after Bart finished his sophomore year at Baylor. When the shooter tried to crawl in through our bathroom window, the alarm went off.

REMAINING QUESTIONS

What would lead a son to do this? Was it hatred? Was it money? Was it only a sick, high-stakes game to see if he was smart enough to outwit everyone? Given human history, it is conceivable to envision a son hating his father, but why would he include his mother and brother?

As strange as it sounds, I do not believe that Bart's motive was hatred. Hatred can be irrational and hard to pin down, but we had never given him any reason to hate us. We had stood with him through the school break-in and trial and had arranged his transfer to a private school so he could start fresh. He had never been abused. Tricia and I had worked hard to raise him with discipline, self-confidence, love, and support. We did many things together: I had coached sports and bicycled nearly twenty thousand miles with him. Tricia volunteered at his school, and we had regular "family fun" evenings. Kevin idolized his big brother, and the two had played well together from early childhood. We had gone on numerous family vacations, and just five months before the shooting, Bart, Kevin, and I had enjoyed those five days of adventure in Colorado. Bart wasn't sullen, angry, or moody when he was around us, although we have since learned that he displayed these characteristics when he was with the dangerous friends he cultivated away from home. He wore one mask when he was with us and another when he was in other situations, and they were well crafted. We didn't realize how split his life had become.

Unlike with Absalom's betrayal, I don't believe Bart's actions stemmed from greed. He got most things he asked for, and he often declined when we offered to buy him things, saying he didn't need them. Also, if money had been his motive, he could have done better by marrying his girlfriend of five years and killing members of her family. They owned a successful business, and their net worth far exceeded ours.

While the police thought it was all about money, I had a private nightmare of another possible explanation. If Bart was actually guilty of this awful crime, was it possible that it was only a wager he had made with himself that he could get away with it? I was reminded of the movie *Trading Places*, in which characters portrayed by Dan Aykroyd and Eddie Murphy were the unwitting participants in a casual wager between two elderly, wealthy brothers—the outcome of which would ruin one young man and elevate the other. Could Bart have been so sick that he might have extinguished our lives and wagered his future on committing this crime and being able to get away with it?

At the time, it was difficult to seriously consider this because I still didn't believe he was involved. However, the thought came unbidden into my mind, and I could not completely rid myself of the haunting possibility. It was the same old Gordian knot: I just didn't have access to the data necessary to choose between believing Bart and believing the police. These fears would sit in the back of my mind for nearly two more years until, late in the summer of 2006, when Bart opened up and I began to understand. I had been wrong about everything.

Chapter 5

INTERLUDES

The first months of 2004 helped both Bart and me reach a new state of normalcy. Things settled into a routine of sorts, and although it wasn't what we had been used to, at least it helped put some order into our chaotic lives. God also chose this time to give me four emotionally healing experiences that spoke strongly to me: he would be with me through all of this; he was still in control; and he was going to bring great good from this horror.

Starting in late January, Bart and I began physical therapy. My wound, in particular, was a mess. When the bullet hit my shoulder, it broke into high-velocity shrapnel that shredded the muscle mass in my chest and upper arm before shattering my humerus bone. I will always have a hollow cavity beneath the bullet hole in my right shoulder, where the tissue was destroyed beyond repair. In the seven weeks from the operation to my first therapy session, my arm had been healing while remaining essentially frozen in place. This immobility led to significant (and potentially permanent) loss in my arm's range of motion, because the interconnective and muscle tissues became fused with scarring. Besides rebuilding muscle mass, the therapy sessions also had to address this problem of inflexibility. The scar tissue had to be painfully stretched and pulled apart before it became too set, or I would spend the rest of my life with a severely restricted and weakened right arm.

All of it was painful, but perhaps the worst part of therapy involved tearing and stretching the scapula tissue. One of the therapists was a huge guy who would have me lie on my stomach as he pried his fingers under my shoulder blade and, so it seemed to me, tried to pull it off. I felt like a Thanksgiving turkey as he yanked and pulled, but fortunately nothing actually got ripped out. He must have known what he was doing because I have become strong again, and my range of motion in that arm is about 80 percent of what it was before the injury.

God's first special gift to remind me that he was there with me occurred in early February, just after I had begun therapy and while my arm was still weak and bound by scar tissue. My brother-in-law (with whom I worked) owned a ranch on about six hundred acres of land between College Station and Huntsville. By that February his herd of cattle had grown to about fifty, and they needed to be wormed and tagged. I will not describe this disgusting procedure except to say that the cows didn't enjoy it much, but it provided some real, down-to-earth cowboy action for us city slickers. The job was a perfect "guys' weekend out" for our company foremen.

We arrived early Saturday morning, and everyone got to work. Although it would drop to nearly freezing at night, temperatures that morning were in the high fifties under grayish skies and a light breeze—just right for the kind of work we were going to do. The plan was to finish by midafternoon and spend the rest of the weekend playing on the four-wheelers, shooting skeet, eating steaks, and generally being rowdy without having to worry about offending any feminine social graces.

There were nine of us: three of our foremen, Ronnie, Reggie, and Travis; Travis's son-in-law, Sam, and Travis's grandson, Cody; Jake, our truck driver; my brother-in-law; me; and Bobby, our sand supplier. With the help of a rancher friend who lived nearby, we rounded up the cattle and were able to get most of them into a holding pen. This pen gradually funneled into a narrow, single-file passageway with a traplike collar at the end. When the collar was closed around the animal's neck, the cow became immobile, and the medicine could be safely applied to its "southern" end. Another buckaroo would log the cow's description, and a third would attach a fashionable yellow plastic earring bearing the cow's number, to ease identification. Once the process was completed, the collar was opened, the cow departed to regain its dignity, and the next one in line got the treatment.

The work wasn't hard, and I did little more than take pictures and tell jokes since my right arm was still essentially useless. But after two hours, we were nearing the end of the job with only four cows yet to be herded into the holding pen. Having grown up around cattle on my grandfather's farm, I saw the problem: Jake and Cody were trying to herd them with four-wheelers, and it wasn't working. So Ronnie, Reggie, and I walked out into the pasture to act as slow-moving human fences. Normally, cattle will allow you to move them around as long as you don't try going too fast; but four-wheelers do not lend themselves to patience.

I was in the middle, and things were going fine until Cody came roaring up and spooked one of the cows. What none of us knew was that this particular cow had just been bought at auction two weeks earlier and had swallowed all the human foolishness she was going to take. Making matters worse, she was purchased pregnant and had given birth to a calf only a week earlier, so her hormones were off the charts. Something snapped inside her, and she attacked Jake's four-wheeler, nearly knocking it over and just missing his leg. He was able to keep two wheels on the ground as he gunned it and pulled away, so she spun around looking for another target . . . and zeroed in on me.

She was about thirty yards away when she charged. It was almost like a cartoon. Her eyes didn't actually turn red, and steam didn't fly from her flared nostrils, but you get the picture. Her eyes, devoid of emotion or intelligence previously, bored into me and communicated perfectly her intentions: *I'm going to kill you!* I remember thinking, *Great. I survive the gunshot only to be gored to death by a mad cow.* What kind of dark cloud was I under? Here she came.

I had about three seconds to decide what to do, which didn't allow much time for elegance in planning. (I am reminded of Arlo Guthrie's attempts at finding a good rhyming word for "motorsickle" as he wrote a song while flying off the side of a mountain on his Harley: sometimes "pickle" is the best you can do with the time you've got.) She was closer to the fence than I was, there wasn't a tree within a hundred yards, and I knew that even being as highly motivated as I was, I could never outrun her. My options were limited, and all I could think of was watching the tiny Olympic gymnasts racing down the lane, hitting the pommel horse with their hands and flipping over it. Although my right arm was very weak, I still figured that if I timed it right, I could grab the horns to keep her from goring or running over me, and push up and off to the right. I would worry about the next pass if I survived the first one. By that time she was there.

The first part of the plan worked fine. I grabbed her horns and jumped backward and away, but I wasn't anywhere near fast or strong enough to avoid being hit. Her broad, bony forehead flew up, slamming me squarely in the chest and launching me into the sky. I went head over heels and landed on my back, knocking the air out of my lungs. Not exactly a 10 on the Olympic scoring system. If she had reached me then, I would have been defenseless.

However, like a well-trained rodeo clown, Jake flew up astride the four-wheeler just in time to get her attention; she rushed after him, which probably saved my life. Ronnie and

Reggie got me up and running toward the fence as fast as possible. Everyone was worried (including me), but I was only badly bruised. I felt like I had been hit by a cow.

We all reached a unanimous decision to leave the lady and her calf alone. If they wanted to get worms, that was their problem.

As strange as it sounds, the "mad cow weekend" gave me great comfort as I realized once again that God can protect us in life-threatening situations.

But protection isn't all he's good at—sometimes he just blesses your socks off, which is what happened with his second gift to me. It came on Kevin's birthday, March 19, 2004.

Each year Houston hosts a three-week livestock show and rodeo that is the largest in the world. Held for years in the Astrodome, it had just moved into new digs at Reliant Stadium, home of the NFL's Houston Texans. Each night, following the rodeo events, a concert is held on a revolving stage in the middle of the arena. Most performances are sold out, which means that when everyone at the midway, rodeo, and livestock exhibitions are totaled up, about seventy thousand people are inside the fences. It's a huge social event, with everyone dressed to the nines in cowboy duds, and everyone loves to go.

Traditionally, our company would buy four nights in one of the skyboxes to entertain clients and employees. When the lineup for performers was announced in 2003 (before the shooting), Kevin came bounding down the stairs in excitement. "Dad! Guess who's playing the rodeo on my birthday! Pat Green! Can we get the skybox for a birthday party?"

Pat Green was Kevin's favorite performer, so I told him I'd see what I could do. Inwardly I figured I would buy a few tickets for him and some friends but that the skybox was out of the question, since the tab runs over a hundred dollars a ticket. When the shooting happened a few weeks later, I forgot all about it. But as we started putting together our company packages in January, I realized that if tickets for that night were still available, I could throw a fantastic birthday party for all of Kevin's friends and honor him in a fun way.

When Acme Brick (from whom we bought the tickets, since they contracted for the whole rodeo) heard why I wanted the skybox that night, they arranged for me to have it even though it was already scheduled for their use. Within a few days I had a guest list that included Bart, his fiancée, and nineteen of Kevin's best friends.

The day of the show, Brittany Barnhill told me she had a surprise. It turned out that one of Pat Green's fraternity brothers went to our church, and when Brittany's dad, Matt, told him about my party, the guy called Pat and got us six backstage passes. I soon found myself with Brittany and four of Kevin's buddies in line to meet the star.

I was genuinely surprised at how gracious he was. Although he was about to perform before fifty thousand people, he took his time and actually visited with everyone who had a backstage pass. He signed autographs, laughed, and posed for pictures. When it was our turn, I told him that twenty-two of us were there celebrating my late son's birthday, and he was sincerely touched. I told him that one of his songs ("Poetry") sounded as if it had been written specifically for

Kevin, and Brittany didn't hesitate to ask Pat if they were going to play it.

"Well, uh, sure! Yeah! We're gonna play it!" He laughed and wrote Kevin's name on his palm with a Magic Marker. We all got pictures taken with him, and then it was back upstairs to watch the rodeo.

When the concert started, the band played three songs, and then Pat announced: "We weren't going to do this song, but I met some folks backstage who asked me to. So, Kevin," he said, pointing up to heaven, "this one's for you!" He launched into "Poetry," and it was all I could do to keep from losing it. The kids fired up the disposable lighters I had bought them, and people all over the stadium saw our skybox light up like a seventies rock show. The review of the performance in the next morning's *Houston Chronicle* even mentioned Pat's song dedication. I wonder if he had any idea how much that meant to us.

The third event that helped me put things back together during those early months was a Texas A&M ceremony in which I had never expected to participate. At a school that honors tradition perhaps more than any other in the country, the ceremony of Muster may be its most sacred. Every year, on San Jacinto Day (which commemorates Texas's independence), Aggies throughout the world hold Muster, reading aloud the name of every Aggie who died that year. When the name is called, another Aggie answers "Here" for the departed, indicating that the bonds of brotherhood forged at A&M are never broken, even by death.

These ceremonies have been held in every military

campaign since World War I, in POW camps, in the jungles of Africa and the crowded metropolises of the world. The largest Muster is always held on campus, in the basketball arena. Twenty thousand Aggies, most of whom have no direct ties to anyone memorialized, come to pay their respects. Although Kevin had spent only two semesters at A&M the previous year, the Muster Committee heard of his death and included him. Once an Aggie, always an Aggie.

A large group, including all of my family, my in-laws, and many friends and people from work, drove up to College Station, and we were treated with the highest respect. Each family was assigned a student who had voluntarily taken hours of special training for the honor of participating in Muster by acting as an escort to the bereaved. They stayed with us throughout the ceremony should any of us need help or attention.

After receiving refreshments, we were taken to the floor of the arena, on which two thousand chairs were set. A single aisle down the middle split them into two large seating areas. I asked Bart to answer for Kevin, and he was given a candle and a place in the front row. Every seat along the perimeter of the floor seats, and those along both sides of the center aisle, held someone with a candle who represented a fallen Aggie. When it came time, each name would be called, going from the youngest Aggie who had died in the previous year to the oldest. Someone representing that person would say "Here" and step forward, lighting his or her candle from the one previously lit, until the lighting around the two areas was complete. When all the candles were lit, both seating sections would be enclosed in a wall of light.

After a couple of speeches, all the lights in the arena were cut, the only illumination being a single candle at the base of the stage. The first name was called, and the sister of a young man killed in Iraq walked to the front and lit a candle for him. Kevin's name was next; Bart answered "Here" and lit his candle from hers. And so the light spread throughout the room as one name after another was called and answered.

By the time the last name was read, hundreds of candles lit up the hushed auditorium. After a long moment of silence, the Ross Volunteers, an elite ceremonial honor group chosen from the entire Corps of Cadets, slowly and silently entered from behind stage right. The honor guard numbered twenty-one riflemen and a leader who whispered the cadence. Their precision was incredible. Because we were seated in the second row, we could hear the leader as he spoke barely audible commands, slowly drawing out each word; I am sure everyone from the fifth row back could hear nothing. Five or six seconds of rigid, immobile silence were followed by the group's suddenly and in perfect precision making the single movement commanded by the leader. More seconds of extended silence preceded the next whispered command, also executed perfectly. It was powerful beyond description.

Several minutes of precise, slow-motion movement passed before the guard was arrayed into three rows of seven, but when they were ready, the leader whispered "Present . . . ar-rrmmms-uh!" in that curiously intoned and drawn-out near-whisper. Nothing happened until suddenly, in one fluid motion, the front row of seven whipped their rifles into position and fired a volley as one shot. The noise was deafening.

Amid the scent of burning candle wax wafted the pungent odor of gunpowder. A moment later the second row fired, and then the third.

After an appropriate period of silent respect, they turned as a single organism and slowly, haltingly, silently reformed and filed out of the hall. It was the most outstanding example of precision work I have ever seen. In fact, the Bryan/College Station phone book featured a picture of the ceremony on its front cover that year. You can clearly see Bart in the front row in his white jacket, with the seven muzzle flashes from the third volley all caught by the camera as they emerged from the guns at the same instant.

These three events, orchestrated by God, showed me several things. The attack by the cow strengthened my faith because it reinforced God's truth about life: as we pass through this fallen world, we will encounter trouble, but God will never leave us, and he can protect us from calamity. The series of coincidences in the rodeo affair were just too many to explain away: Kevin's favorite performer playing on his birthday; gaining access to the skybox even though it had already been reserved; Pat Green's friend attending our church and hearing of the situation; receiving the passes; our meeting the star and my unplanned comment about "Poetry"; and then Pat changing his set list at the last minute. All of these happened so that he could dedicate the song to Kevin in front of fifty thousand people in that stadium. This string of events convinces me that God orders the details of our lives and gives us blessings. The Muster ceremony was a reminder that even in the midst of loss and grieving, beauty exists, no one is forgotten, and others will help to carry the load—even people we do not know.

Yet perhaps the most moving of my four experiences centered on a bicycle ride. For years we had a wonderful neighbor who was also the most gifted dentist I've ever met. But to look at him, you would think he was a mountain man lost in suburbia. "Dr. Rod" would be in overalls or jeans whenever he was home, and with his full beard and sandals, it would have been easy to underestimate him or mistake him for a character in the movie *Deliverance*. Bart idolized him and thought he was the coolest neighbor. When Rod got sick and suffered mysterious and sudden muscle deterioration, leading to the loss of his dental practice, it devastated ten-year-old Bart.

One day Bart mentioned seeing a sign for a bicycle ride from Houston to Austin, called the MS150, that raised money to fight multiple sclerosis. No one knew what Rod had, but MS was a possibility, and Bart wanted to ride for him. I tried to talk him out of it because I knew that if he rode, I was going to have to ride too—and I definitely wasn't interested in going that far on a bicycle. But he stubbornly persisted because he wanted to do something for Rod. I finally decided that the best way to convince him of the impossibility of riding 180 miles on a bicycle was to do a thirty-mile training ride and let him see for himself. But instead of scaring him, it fanned the flames; so when the next spring came around, we set out on our first two-day bike ride.

We grew to love the sport, and this would be just the first of thirteen MS150s in which I rode (most of them with Bart) before the shooting and a herniated disk in my neck sidelined my cycling career. With all the training rides we did together, we both became quite good, and two years in a row Bart was the fastest of the more than a hundred riders thirteen years of age or younger. Also during this time Bart and I became active in the ride's coordination, both holding positions as Ride Marshals (Bart being the youngest ever accepted). I served for eleven years on the ride's Steering Committee. As one of the committee chairmen for the ride, I often ran into planning problems that called for help from the local MS Society chapter, and my favorite go-to gal was Kelli Boltz.

Kelli is one of those rare people who never get flustered and can think of solutions no one else sees. I always looked to her first when I needed help, because I knew she would not only figure out a solution but follow through with it. We talked often about many subjects, and so I learned that she was not at all interested in "religious things." On those occasions when I shared my faith with her, I could tell she was just being polite as she listened. Then one day she was no longer on staff, but none of us volunteers knew why. A year later Kevin and Tricia died, and as a result of my injuries, I was unable to train or ride the MS150 when it took place the weekend before Muster.

On the Friday night before the ride's Saturday morning start, I decided at the last minute to go to the big Bike Expo held at the ride's official hotel. Thousands of people would be there, especially since the ride had now grown to more than ten thousand riders. I spent an hour and a half visiting with friends and had many people tell me how sorry they were and how much they missed me. So when I left around nine o'clock., I was already "feeling the love."

Passing through the dark and packed parking lot, I stepped between two of the many cars slowly circling, looking for a space. Suddenly the passenger door of the car I had stepped in front of swung open and a woman rushed toward me, screaming, "Kent! Kent!" Kelli was almost crying as she hugged me. Eventually her story came out, as she and I visited in the hotel parking lot.

Kelli had left the MS office because of differences with her boss and had harbored bitterness about it. After the shooting, she attended the funeral, though I hadn't seen her in the crowd. The service moved her greatly, since she knew both Tricia and me, and when she walked out of the church that morning, she took an honest look at her life and saw a lot of emptiness. She realized that one day she would die, and she wanted what Tricia and Kevin had: a legacy of service and commitment to others and an assurance that she would go to heaven. For three weeks she wrestled with this, and one day while dropping her son off for day care at a Methodist church, she picked up a pamphlet for a women's Bible study. Remembering my talks with her, she finally understood why she needed a relationship with God, and she asked Jesus to be her Lord and Savior. Her life began changing almost immediately.

One of the biggest changes came when she realized that she needed to forgive those with whom she had differed at the MS office. She decided to ride that year and see all her old friends and coworkers, hence her dropping by the Bike

Expo that evening. Afterward, she told me that the ride was a wonderful experience and that she had needed to forgive to be freed from the bitterness that had only been hurting her. She felt liberated.

Other changes came as well. Growing hungry to serve others, she has been on two mission trips to Central America, she's become active in her church, and she and her partner of ten years (who had undergone a separate but powerful experience with God on the same day Kelli had!) rededicated their lives to Jesus and were officially married.

That night in the parking lot, she told me how her life had been changed for the better because she had seen how the gospel had been lived out in Tricia's and Kevin's lives and how I had responded to the news media after the shooting. It all clicked together, and she understood what I had tried to explain three years earlier.

None of this would have happened without the shooting. And I might never have known about the impact those events had on Kelli's and her husband's lives. I suspect there will be many other stories like hers, but I may not learn of them until I get to heaven. I'm grateful that God let me learn of this one. He not only directed my going to the Expo when I hadn't planned to but also timed my movements so I would pass right into the headlight glow of the people he knew needed to see me.

Taken together, these four interludes not only helped me through this most difficult time but also displayed God's love and character. I think God gave me these gifts—these beautiful memories and powerful experiences (which all happened within a few weeks)—because he knew that the coming months were going to test me in ways I could never imagine. He wanted me to understand that he was there to walk with me as I traveled the hard roads ahead and that he had a purpose behind what was coming.

Chapter 6

HITTING THE FAN

With all the sudden changes that had occurred in my life, you'd think I would be better prepared for the inevitable next round. But on June 7, 2004, I was caught off guard when the police finally moved out of the background and took center stage.

For years Tricia and I had been active supporters of a local charity called Second Mile Mission Center. Second Mile had rapidly become one of the largest and most effective benevolences in southwest Houston, providing free food, clothing, and other services to forty thousand clients per year. One of the mission's fund-raisers was a spring golf tournament, and as a member of the board, I was present on the evening of that event to help with the dinner and silent auction held afterward. As the meal was coming to a close, my cell phone rang. It was police detective Marshall Slot.

"Kent, we need to talk, and soon. You are still living with Bart, right? I'm worried about your safety. Can you come to the station tomorrow?"

As usual, when Marshall popped unexpectedly into my life, my heart raced and my stomach turned over. He always seemed to have bad news.

"What's wrong? Have you learned something?"

"I don't want to talk about it over the phone, but I would like to go over where we stand in the case. Can you come in?"

Thinking that details might now be forthcoming, I told him I would call him in a day or two. He told me not to wait.

The next morning I called Bart's attorney, Dan Cogdell, to get his input. Dan believed the police didn't have anything new, that they were just trying to create conflict between Bart and me, but that I should meet with them to see if I could learn anything. He said that since he was Bart's attorney and not mine, he couldn't represent me, but he suggested I get an attorney and meet the police in a neutral location. He gave me the names of two or three respected lawyers in the area, and I retained one.

On Thursday, June 10 (the six-month anniversary of the shooting), I went by Tricia's and Kevin's grave sites for a few minutes, then drove back to Sugar Land for my meeting with Marshall. He brought his partner with him, and the four of us talked for two hours in my attorney's office. I felt like the target in some arcade game.

It was all just more of the same. They knew terrible things but they couldn't give me details. I was in great danger. I needed to withdraw my support for Bart. The one new thing I heard was that they claimed to have found another planned attempt on the family that had failed, but they gave me no details to check. I told them again that I wasn't discounting their claims but that I had lived with Bart for half a year since the shooting, and if he had wanted to harm me, he'd had plenty of chances. Furthermore, while I was not siding with him, I wouldn't dismiss Bart's claims of innocence unless the police could give me some basis for believing them. All I got was more vague assertions that they knew he was responsible for the shootings. Perhaps they couldn't share details because the investigation was still ongoing, but I felt that surely they could offer some proof, especially since Marshall had implied over the phone that they would. I left shaking inside because there seemed to be no way to resolve the conflict I had faced for so long. Since I didn't know whom to believe, I could only remain neutral and wait for something to happen. On the way home, I decided not to mention the meeting to anyone, especially Bart. I would just keep my eyes open. How I wished I could have talked to Tricia! She was the one person with whom I felt safe to share anything.

What I did know was that Bart's wedding would be in six weeks, and God needed to do something fast to clear up the question of guilt or innocence. The police had been quiet for a long time, and I had come to think they might be giving up pursuing Bart for lack of evidence; but after this meeting, it was obvious that they were even more entrenched.

What if they were right? What if there had been previous plots, if the Waco incident had been real? I couldn't let the wedding take place if I thought it would put Bart's fiancée or any of her family in danger. If Bart was guilty of arranging our murders, I couldn't let him be in a position to inherit some of her family's estate. As long as he remained unmarried, there was little advantage for him should one of her family members die. I felt that everyone was safe until the nuptials on July 24.

For more than a week nothing happened. Then, on Friday afternoon, Bart's fiancée called me.

"Mr. Whitaker, have you talked to the police?"

Instantly, I saw what was happening. The police knew that in the Waco incident Bart had been isolated, had become afraid, and had run. If Bart were to flee now, whether they caught him or not, they would win, because in the eyes of the public Bart would be guilty—an innocent man doesn't run under suspicion. If they did catch him, Bart's plea of innocence would be discounted. Either way, the prosecution came out ahead. Even if no real evidence existed against Bart (and I still knew nothing of the strength of their investigation), they would win if he disappeared, because they would never have to try the case and face cross-examination that might cause weak arguments to unravel. In that light, it made strategic sense for them to try to separate Bart from all support. I reasoned that their first move was to try to get me to turn on Bart so that he might grow afraid and run away; when that didn't happen, they turned to his fiancée. As sensitive and sweet as she was, I feared that she would fall apart if they pounded on her like they had me. I tried to downplay the meeting.

"Yeah, it was just more of the same old thing. They didn't tell me anything new; just tried to scare me. Did they call you too?"

"Yes, and I am scared. They said I was in danger, and I should not be alone with him. They want to meet with me right away!"

So now they wanted to meet with her. Shifting gears, I decided to face the problem head-on.

"Listen, they're trying to scare us. They didn't tell me anything new, but you know how they are: they will beat you down with arguments without backing anything up with details. You can't go to that meeting alone. I'll go with you if you like, or better yet, get your dad. And a lawyer. You'll need someone there to watch out for you. Can you stop by my house tonight on your way home and talk about it?"

So while Bart was at work, she and I discussed everything. She promised to tell her dad, consider getting an attorney, and put off the police as long as possible before making an appointment.

After a week and a half, the real lightning struck.

On Tuesday, June 23, Dan Cogdell called and wanted Bart and me to come to his office the next morning. When we arrived, he got right to the point: while in Fort Bend the previous day, he had run into one of the investigators on the case for the Sugar Land police. Dan's account of their conversation rocked me to the core.

"He asked if I had talked to Bart recently, and I told him that I had not and asked if there was some reason." Dan continued, "He told me that they [the police] knew about the wedding coming up and told me that they were going to 'destroy Bart's life' and that 'the wedding will never take place.'" According to Dan, those were the officer's actual words.

Once that sank in, Bart and I talked, but he had retreated behind his emotional armor. Although I couldn't tell what was going on inside his head, I cautioned him to hold fast and promised that I would be with him through it all. Outwardly he agreed. We considered the possibility that an arrest might take place soon, but that they might actually wait to do it until the day of the wedding. I tried to put myself in Bart's shoes, imagining that horrible scene: standing in a tux at the front of the church, family and friends gathered there along with the love of his life, only to be arrested in front of everyone. I could find no words to describe how that would feel.

I repeatedly emphasized that he had to stay and face this, not like what happened in Waco. If he ran, they would win because they would never have to defend any of their charges. Bart would be on the run for the rest of his life, and that wouldn't be easy in this day of computers and high-tech methods of tracking and identification. He agreed to stand firm and face what was coming, including telling his fiancée's parents and our family of the police's intentions. The storm clouds that had been building on the horizon for so long were now swirling around us.

That evening, and again the following day, Bart and I made plans. He would arrange a meeting for us with his fiancée's family on Monday or Tuesday and with my and Tricia's families on the following days. It was imperative that everyone be warned that Bart might be arrested. Decisions had to be made about postponing or canceling the wedding. Bart seemed to be focused and resigned to fighting the accusations, ready to do whatever needed to be done to get through this ordeal.

On Sunday evening, June 27, at about eight o'clock, I was upstairs exercising when Bart came to tell me good night. He said he was meeting some friends at a club and that he would be going to work early the next morning, so he probably would stay at his fiancée's house that night, since it was so close to work. I told him good-bye and that I loved him, and went back to working out. He went downstairs, out the front door . . . and was gone without contact for fifteen months.

How I wish I had stopped exercising and hugged him, as I often did when we parted. I didn't know it then, but it was the last chance I would ever have to touch him, to hug him. I just didn't take the time, and now we'll never get closer than opposite sides of bulletproof glass.

The next morning I had just arrived at work when I received a call from a Houston policeman who asked if I owned a 2001 Yukon. I replied that it was my son's vehicle, and the officer told me it was in an apartment parking lot with the door open and the engine running. I almost panicked, because I instantly knew in my heart of hearts that Bart had run. Putting the officer on hold, I tried to reach Bart first on his cell phone (no answer) and then by calling the restaurant where he worked. The manager told me that Bart was not scheduled to work that day, which contradicted what Bart had told me the night before. I tried his cell phone again and still got no answer, so I left a frantic message to call me as soon as possible; then I got back on the phone with the officer. I told him that I had been unable to reach Bart. He suggested that since the apartment complex had a history of criminal activity, he would turn off the engine and lock the keys inside the SUV. Since I would be able to get in with a second set of keys, that's what we agreed to do.

I called Dan, who felt we should keep this quiet for a day or two, giving Bart a chance to come to his senses and return. He had not yet been charged with anything or told to advise the police of any movements out of the area, and no one else knew he was gone; it would be best for us to look for him first. If we could find him before the Sugar Land police learned of his disappearance, no one would have to know about it. Besides, I couldn't legally report him missing yet because police procedures require that an adult be missing for at least twenty-four hours before a report can be filed. We would give him some time. If he didn't return, we would call a news conference and ask for help in locating him.

My brother-in-law followed me home from work to get the spare keys; he then took me to the apartment building, and we found the Yukon without any trouble. Opening it, I saw that the console and glove box had been ransacked, and papers were everywhere. I took some pictures and then drove it home. I had the desperate feeling that I would never see my son again. Walking into the empty house, I realized just how alone I was. The grief welled up in me so fiercely that I fell apart, crying out, "I am totally alone! They're all gone! All of them!" and sat down on the stairs and cried for the first time in weeks. It was horrible. I felt like an abandoned orphan. The isolation that the police had tried to create in Bart had instead found me. I couldn't imagine trying to face everything with all of my family gone. I felt like David must have felt when he learned that his son Absalom was dead.

People have asked me why I didn't call the police at once, in case Bart had been a victim of foul play. But somehow I knew that he wasn't injured, that abandoning the Yukon had been planned. It occurred to me that if he was trying to run away, this would be a good ploy. If someone in the seedy complex saw the SUV open and running, they might steal it, and a chop shop would break it down into untraceable parts within hours, obscuring his trail. If someone stole it and was later caught by police, the authorities would not believe their story of finding it with the engine running and would want to know what had happened to Bart. And if it was just found with the door open and engine running, it would at least provide a short-term smoke screen. Whatever happened, it would buy him some time to disappear.

I was pulled in two directions because I still didn't know whether Bart was innocent or not. I felt guilty for not calling the police right away because I had promised them many times I would if anything happened. He hadn't been charged with anything and had every right to leave if he chose, but I wished desperately that he hadn't done so, especially without leaving me a way to contact him. His actions were incriminating, and I realized that they were causing me to shift away from my neutrality: I now believed that he was somehow involved in the deaths of Tricia and Kevin. Was he Absalom in disguise? I was about two-thirds convinced that the police were right. Even so, in my weakness I couldn't call them without giving him a chance to return on his own.

The next evening (Tuesday), Dan and I met with Bart's fiancée's family and told them what had happened. They were shocked, and although encouraging and upbeat toward me, underneath was an understandable sense of anger, betrayal, and disbelief. They left after an hour and a half, but I suspect that they all met again at one of their homes to continue the discussion privately.

The next night Dan and I met with my family. As with the previous meeting, there was disbelief and shock. My sister in particular was adamant that Bart couldn't be involved, saying that with all the unfair things happening to him, she didn't blame him for running away. But by the end of the evening, everyone had accepted the truth: Bart had fled, and this gave credence to the possibility that he really had been involved in the slaying of his own family. While we could continue to pray for his return, we knew to expect a news storm any moment, as the story either leaked out or we made an announcement. Everyone stood with me, promising that whatever happened, they loved us both, and if Bart was guilty, they prayed that he would be captured soon so we could find out why this had happened and he could start receiving the help he needed.

The next few days were hard because I had to pretend nothing was wrong. I called Bart's workplace and told them he had gone out of town unexpectedly and wouldn't be back on rotation for at least a week. On Friday evening I met with seven of Kevin's friends for an evening of pizza and catching up. Afterward, I asked Brittany Barnhill (who was still depressed after the murders) to stay for a few minutes, and I talked with her about moving on—and with every word of encouragement to her I was reminded of the parallels in my life and how badly I missed Kevin too. And Tricia. And now Bart.

A month earlier, four of Kevin's close friends had called, saying they had something they wanted to show me. All four arrived in shorts and sandals, and as they stepped into the entryway where Kevin had died, they lined up in chorus-line fashion, with their right feet out in front. On the inside of each of their right ankles was a tattoo of an ichthus (the fish symbol for Christianity), just like Kevin had gotten the previous spring at A&M. But whereas Kevin's tattoo had a cross inside the fish's outline, in their tattoos the cross was on top, with the initials "KW" where the fish's eye would have been. I was blown away. I told them they were all boneheads, but I loved it, and when I joked that I might get one too, they announced that Brittany was planning to get one. As soon as the boys left, I called Matt, and he told me he had heard about it and had tried to talk her out of getting the tattoo.

"Brittany, we all loved Kevin, but one day you will marry someone. What is your husband going to think when he finds that you have the initials of another man tattooed on your leg?"

"Well, Dad," she had replied, "he'll just have to get used to it!"

Typical feisty Brittany—and knowing her, she meant it.

So on this Friday evening after the other friends had left and Brittany remained (and as I struggled to hide the news of Bart's disappearance), I talked to her about the future, the permanence of tattoos, and Kevin. She agreed to wait six months and see how she felt then about getting a tattoo. As she drove away, I heaved a sigh of relief, both for her decision and that I had been able to keep quiet about Bart's disappearance.

On Monday night, with still no word from Bart, his fiancée's stepmom called to say that they had decided over the Fourth of July weekend to send out wedding cancellation notices. I was heartbroken but agreed it was the only thing to do. I called Dan to inform him of their decision and my wish to send out e-mail notices to my friends as well. We agreed that there was no point in putting it off any longer: he would call a press conference.

Two things happened on Wednesday morning, July 7, 2004. First, Dan announced to the media that Bart was gone and that I would file a missing persons report with the police later that day. We were asking for help in finding him and were hoping that he would hear the broadcast and return as soon as possible. The phone calls from the news media flooded in, both to Dan's office and my home, with everyone wanting to know if I thought Bart was guilty and why he had run.

The second thing that happened was that a Harris County grand jury indicted Ken Lay, former chairman of the infamously failed Enron Corporation, charging him with multiple counts of fraud.

As big as the Sugar Land murders were in the Houston area, Ken Lay's indictment was big-time national news, so the media concentrated on that story instead. Now that they had a much bigger fish to fry, our story was demoted to second largest of the week, and I was spared several days of intensive harassment.

Even so, we were still an important enough story to receive at least two minutes with background and multiple reporters on all of the five local television stations. In fact, before the five o'clock evening news came on, I was lucky enough to spot a mobile unit pulling into our cul-de-sac. I dropped everything and headed for the car. By the time I left the house, two other units had arrived and were setting up cameras, but I was gone before they were ready. I phoned Matt, and he, Brittany, and I ate supper together at a Mexican restaurant, then went back to their house.

About nine o'clock, figuring that the vultures must have gone back to their stations, I headed home but on the way called a neighbor to confirm that the coast was clear. She told me the pack was still there; the whole cul-de-sac was full of media mobile units. I reasoned that they wanted footage for the ten o'clock news, so I sat at a gas station for an hour before trying again. By then the reporters had cleared out, and with Enron to occupy them, I wasn't bothered again for some time. Thank you, Ken Lay.

Chapter 7

CLEANING UP THE MESS

Two days after announcing Bart's disappearance, I got the first of many notices that he was behind in paying his bills, especially bills relating to his house, which he hadn't lived in since the shooting. He had become inconsistent in paying or had skipped paying such things as homeowners insurance, annual property taxes, utility bills, homeowners' association dues, Visa charges, and a City of Houston traffic citation. As with many college students, he received mail at both his current address and his family's permanent address, so some of the termination notices—and the warning that a warrant for his arrest was imminent because of the unpaid ticket—came to my house.

Well, good luck getting paid, I thought. Wondering how many other bills were out there that I didn't know about, I made the ninety-mile drive to his home and tried to get into the locked mailbox. But since it had been clogged with mail and obviously unattended for months, the carrier had long ago pulled everything, and then the post office had lost it or thrown it all away. I asked the post office to forward all new mail from his home address to mine. It would be months before I stopped getting past-due notices.

I almost let everything default, but finally I decided to pay the bills as I found them. The house was empty, and if Bart didn't return soon, it would be impossible to sell without electricity, water, taxes, and insurance paid to date. Also, I didn't like the idea of someone else getting stiffed because my son was irresponsible, even if it was some huge, faceless corporation. Fortunately, months earlier I had taken the precautionary measure of getting Bart's power of attorney; without it, paying his bills would have been nearly impossible. Even armed with that legal document, it was like pulling teeth because no one wanted to release his financial information. It was an ironic catch-22: I was trying to pay for obligations that would otherwise have to be written off, yet couldn't get the creditors to give me specific amounts or account numbers so I could do it!

During this time I grew very angry at Bart for deserting me like this. Commitments are serious things to me, and I couldn't understand how he could be so cavalier about them. His lack of regard for others cast doubt on his sincerity and innocence, making it a lot harder for me to continue giving him the benefit of the doubt.

Detective Slot capitalized on my growing fears by constantly pointing out Bart's shortcomings and failures. A week after we announced that Bart had disappeared, he went to my parents' home to inspect the abandoned Yukon. I had taken the vehicle to their house the day after Dan and I told my family Bart was gone because I wanted it away from Sugar Land. It wouldn't do for anyone to ask why Bart's SUV was always at my house, so I took it where no one would recognize it.

As Marshall looked through the cluttered vehicle, he asked questions about Bart and whether he had a history of irresponsible behavior. I had to admit that there'd been times when Bart had failed to honor commitments, but always with plausible excuses that were followed by the problem being corrected. And honestly, for every such incident I knew of, I could give dozens of examples when he'd acted responsibly. Still, I wondered if Tricia and I had been too quick to accept excuses and overlook things. I was growing fearful that I might have been fooled—not only in this but in other areas as well. It is so difficult to know the truth when someone as skilled as Bart wants to keep you blind. I realized once again that I might be a father on a terrible journey, waking up to the truth that I had been living with a son who had slipped into darkness without my knowing it. It was becoming clear that my son had a side that none of our family had seen, and I was furious, hurt, and worried about how far the deception had gone.

My dad, who had joined us outside, became agitated as he listened to Marshall's hard questions. The shooting had affected him in a profound way. Even though he was in his eighties, he had been active and robust prior to the murders; but Tricia's and Kevin's deaths and Bart's possible involvement had withered him. He had grown old in a short time. The idea that his model grandson might be responsible for this worst of nightmares was more than he could process, and he became upset every time the topic came up.

On this day his grief and broken heart were aggravated afresh, and he spoke with barely controlled emotion of his experience as a member of three grand juries. As a loyal supporter of the police community, it tore him up to consider Bart's involvement, especially since he couldn't understand why the police wouldn't give us a few details about the man who killed himself the night of the murders or about the girl who had wanted to leave her boyfriend. Marshall explained that they had looked into both leads and found no basis for further investigation; but again he would give no specifics as to why these were dead ends. He finally left, and I was able to calm Dad down a bit.

I would later learn the strength of the case against Bart and that Marshall already knew the answers to some of the questions he asked us that day. I also would learn what a good job Marshall and the police had done on the investigation. But at this point, my family was still in the dark. It was extremely frustrating.

A week later I received a much-needed blessing. Our company insurance agent and fellow FAT man, Jim Frith, called me.

"Hey, buddy, are you busy Wednesday morning? Think you can get away from work for a week? I just had a client cancel on me at the last minute. How would you like to take his place in Alaska, fly-fishing for fifty-pound king salmon?"

I have had strange and unexpected phone calls before, but that has to rank in the top ten. "Gosh, let me check my busy schedule: Well, I did have a wedding during that time, but it seems to have been canceled. And my birthday falls right at the start of the trip, so I would have to postpone supper at Mom's, but I guess I could work it in . . . Are you kidding?! When do we leave?"

The more I learned of the trip, the more fantastic it sounded. Our group would be made up of six guests and three guides. We would fly into Anchorage, then board a float plane (something I had always dreamed of doing) and fly to Alaska's interior, spending five nights camping along a small river full of salmon. The trip would take us through sixty-five miles of wilderness, stopping at three campsites.

Forty hours later we took off, passing westward through three time zones and spending what felt like an interminable six and a half hours on the plane. When we finally arrived in Anchorage, where we would spend the night before leaving for the interior early the following morning, I was surprised at the temperate weather and the explosion of color and perfume from the flowers that were everywhere. It would be freezing in a few months, and the world-famous Iditarod dogsled race would begin at this same hotel, but now we could enjoy the mild Alaskan summer. We ate supper outside on the hotel's patio, comfortable in short sleeves. When we turned in at about ten o'clock, it was still light outside.

The next morning we tromped down to breakfast in our

waders, carrying our big yellow dry bags that held everything we would use for six days. On the shuttle van to the air taxi hangar, we were told we would have to wait two hours for the fog up-country to clear. This gave us time to wander around and be amazed.

Anchorage stretches around a lake and a bay that opens onto the Pacific Ocean, and I think every inch of its perimeter had a float plane on it. It seemed nearly everybody had one, since most places in Alaska have no road access; the only way in or out is cross-country by four-wheel drive or air. Or dogsled. In the winter, when the lakes are frozen over, pilots replace the planes' pontoons with giant skis or balloon tires for landing on ice.

In terms of float planes, the Beaver we flew was the mama bear—there are lots of smaller ones, and one model bigger, but the Beaver was the pack mule used by most outfitters. Still, to us it seemed small, with a total payload (including six passengers, a pilot, and our gear) of about 1,750 pounds. It was also sixty years old, since these planes haven't been built since the 1950s, and every part except the engine block was probably a third-generation replacement. The tight seating arrangements made the economy seats we had complained about from Houston seem palatial. Nobody cared; five minutes after the smooth-as-glass takeoff, we were flying a thousand feet above Alaskan wilderness. What an awesome way to spend my birthday!

A little over an hour later, we set down on the beautiful waters of Chelatna Lake in the southwest corner of Denali National Park, met our guides, and boarded two inflatable rafts.

After a leisurely three-hour trip, we reached our campsite and broke out the fishing gear.

God showed his sense of humor when he allowed me (the least experienced fisherman in the group) to net the first salmon of the trip. Another great birthday present! The fact that I didn't net another one for a day and a half, however, kept me humble. As time passed I become frustrated, wondering what I needed to do to actually reel in another salmon and not just hook it for a minute or two. I grew morose and began thinking about my life and how it seemed to be paralleling the life cycle of these huge fish.

Everyone knows that salmon hatch in freshwater streams and then spend most of their lives in salt water once they're swept into the ocean by spring floods. But most folks don't know what happens when the salmon return to their spawning grounds. Over the years, as they feed on the bounties of the Pacific Ocean, they grow large, often reaching forty or fifty pounds. But at some point they exchange that good life to answer God's call to reproduce, which can only happen in the small tributary where their own egg was hatched. Don't ask me how they know where to go, but they do, and they'll fight their way upstream hundreds of miles to get there. Along the way, as they pass from the ocean's salt water to the freshwater lakes and streams, their bodies undergo a strange change: the reemergence into fresh water triggers the closing of a flap in their throat that prevents them from swallowing. They are now on a one-way trip to starvation, hoping only to reach their spawning grounds before they die.

As isolated as we were, I still felt an overwhelming desire

to be alone with my thoughts, so I waded back to shore and walked into the thick brush along the river. I felt a close sympathy with the salmon on their sad trip of death as I fought my way up life's river, hopelessly lost in a world of grief. I thought about Bart's fiancée and her family, about to live through the day of the wedding that would never happen. I desperately missed Bart and wondered where he was. I thought about how much I missed Tricia and Kevin and that for the first time in my life I was spending my birthday without any family. Then I was quietly crying.

I remembered the last big fish I had seen caught, when our family vacationed in Cancún two years earlier. Kevin loved to fish, so we went deep-sea fishing for half a day. He hooked a huge barracuda, which fought for twenty minutes before we got it aboard. It measured a spectacular sixty-nine inches, and Kevin (who often downplayed his achievements) was ecstatic when the captain said that they saw a fish like that only seven or eight times a year. I thought how much Kevin would have loved this trip to Alaska and how Bart would have loved the photography opportunities and the laughing and storytelling. Tricia wouldn't have come for anything. No toilets! No hot water! No hair dryer or telephone! But she would have been tickled pink if her three guys had come. Now my family was all gone. It was just me. I felt desolate.

Suddenly I was aware that Frith and Paul Hicks (another FAT-man friend who had come on the trip) were there, hugging my shoulders. Nobody said much, but before long I felt less alone and realized again that through this whole ordeal, God had placed friends and experiences in my life to help me. After a while I let out a long breath, and we rejoined the world.

That trip was a magic-carpet ride that allowed me to escape for a while. The scenery was beautiful, and we made many amazing memories. On the third morning, we floated downstream for several hours to what became my favorite camping spot. I had gotten better at casting and judging whether the bump at the end of the line was a rock or a fish. The salmon were stacked pretty deep as they rested, and I began catching them again. Even the scenery was bigger than life. As I stood thigh-deep in cold, rushing water, Mt. McKinley (known by the Athabasca Indians as Denali—"the great one") gazed down the middle of the river at us from at least fifty miles away. Spectacular, capped with snow even in late July, the mountain was impossibly big. Our weather was perfect: days in the upper sixties with clear skies, light winds, and no other people. It was a place for the heart to heal. But as the Darling children in *Peter Pan* learned, you can't stay in Neverland. Eventually, you have to leave.

The trip back was uneventful, but I knew that I was returning to real life and would again face the task of climbing my own impossible mountain.

Chapter 8

THE WORST DAY OF MY LIFE

Not long after my return from Alaska, I realized that my job at the construction company was too fast-paced to allow me to heal. Grief takes over your whole life, and it doesn't just evaporate; you need to pass through every one of its dark rooms, and that takes time and effort. I needed to be more still and let God work on my battered soul, so I considered how I might accomplish this and still prepare for the next chapter in my life.

Cliff Parker had been a friend for years and was a member of the FAT-men group. Three years earlier he had left his position as president of an information technology firm, and he and his wife committed to feeding and clothing the poor in

Fort Bend County. They expanded a part-time Sunday-school program into Second Mile Mission Center and began providing free assistance to the large percentage of county citizens below the poverty level. Their ministry had grown to be the largest Houston Food Bank partner in west Houston, providing more than forty thousand clients a year with free food, clothing, medical assistance, housewares, and other services.

As a member of their board of directors, I knew what a good job they were doing with the assets they had but that the need greatly exceeded their means. Now that I had no family to support, it seemed God was nudging me to leave the world of commercial construction and to work with Cliff at Second Mile as a full-time volunteer. I would help to raise funds and pursue grants. If I was successful, perhaps the budget would grow to include a salary for me. It seemed like a perfect answer: I could concentrate on helping others while slowing down a lot and letting God help me. So at the end of 2004 I left the construction company, and for the first time in forty years, I didn't bring home a paycheck. But things wouldn't stay quiet for long—another emotional Vesuvius was just waiting to erupt.

About ten o'clock one morning, trouble walked back into my life.

I had settled into my full-time volunteering job at Second Mile, and many months had passed since the police had interrupted my quiet existence. I'd grown used to the relative peace. That changed when the front desk attendant at Second Mile informed me that detective Marshall Slot and his partner, Billy Baugh, wanted to see me.

The officers entered my tiny office, closing the door behind them. We exchanged brief pleasantries. Then Marshall handed me a sheet of paper.

"Kent, this is a subpoena, and it calls you to testify before the grand jury next week. They'll be asking questions about everything: the night of the shooting, your relationship with Bart, his disappearance, any contact with Bart, and whatever else the district attorney might want to ask. Based on all the grand jury testimony and the police reports, the panel will then vote on whether to bring charges against any potential suspects.

"As you know, a grand jury is different from all other types of court appearances because it's held in secret. There will be no media to record the proceedings, and it is run by the district attorney, not a judge. You cannot have a lawyer present, and afterward, you can't talk about anything that happens in the testimony; nor can you take notes. In fact, you cannot even tell anyone that you are going to a grand jury."

As always, Marshall spoke quietly and with compassion; but the hard walls of my tiny little office seemed to bounce the words around, making me feel attacked from all sides.

The prospect was intimidating, even though I had nothing to hide, because I knew little about how things worked in the legal system. I didn't know what rights I had (if any) or how the game was played. I badly needed some general information so I would know what to expect. Since my dad had served as a member of several grand juries in Houston, I asked the detectives if I could talk to him. They told me I couldn't tell anyone about the subpoena—not my lawyer, not my parents, not even my boss at Second Mile; I could only tell him that I would be gone for much of that day.

When I arrived home that evening, I looked up "grand jury" in the encyclopedia and learned a few things. For one, grand juries have a lot of power. They meet without any type of media oversight, and their job is to review the evidence and decide if it's sufficient to bring charges against someone. In this, their knowledge base would be far ahead of mine, since I still didn't know what the police had found in their investigation. I only knew that they had been quiet for many months. Did the subpoena mean that they had uncovered incriminating new evidence, or did it mean that the district attorney had no real case and was merely rolling the dice, hoping the circumstantial evidence against Bart would be enough to coax an indictment from the grand jury? Was Bart guilty, or was he just a handy scapegoat? I was not comforted when I read that the system is opposed by many people who charge that too often the jury follows the prosecutor's wishes without fully considering the evidence.

On the appointed day I arrived at the courthouse around eight thirty in the morning and eventually found parking on a side street about three blocks away. After praying for several minutes, I got out of my car feeling that I was as ready as I could be.

The Fort Bend County Courthouse is located in historic Richmond, Texas, a little town about twenty minutes from my home. An old domed building, it houses courtrooms and offices jutting off the circular floor plan. The hearing would be on the second level, across the rotunda from the courtroom in which Bart had pleaded guilty to breaking into his high school six years earlier. As I approached the building, walking under the stately boughs of centuries-old pecan and oak trees, I wondered how many parents over the last 150 years had made that stressful march under the same peaceful trees. Entering through the side door, I found that the vestibule downstairs was nearly empty, and no one paid any attention to me. Good. I'd get in there and back out by lunch. My footsteps echoed on the black-and-white tiles as I hurried up the spiral staircase. Reaching the landing, I stepped around the corner and was assaulted.

Intense light stabbed at my eyes. Three camera crews leaped forward. Through the glare all I saw were lenses and reporters, as they shoved microphones in front of my face and shot rapid-fire questions at me.

"Mr. Whitaker, is your son guilty?"

"Do you know where Bart is?"

"What can you tell us about what happened that night?"

"Why have you been called to testify?"

I've seen film clips of animals frozen into immobility when caught in the white blaze of headlights. I can identify with that helpless feeling. At first, there was too much input for my senses, and I stood transfixed, with an idiotic expression on my face, trying to process this ambush. Then I realized what was happening, and all I wanted was to be alone so I could think. I forced my way through the encircling sharks, searching for some kind of sanctuary. An elderly man with a clipboard stood next to a sign: GRAND JURY IN SESSION. QUIET PLEASE. I headed for him.

"Are you here to testify for the grand jury? Here, sign on this line and take a place on the benches. You will be called when it's your turn," the proctor said, indicating a single row of benches along the edge of the room I had just crossed. The thought of being a sitting target for all the cameras was more than I could take.

"I cannot sit out there!" I said as three cameras crowded around, recording my every word. "You've got to find me someplace away from them!" In my naïveté I barked that it wasn't fair—the proceedings were supposed to be secret. How had the media found out? Had someone within the system tipped them off?

The man either took pity on me or he read the rising anger in my eyes. I had played by the rules and talked to no one about the subpoena, even though I desperately needed help to fight off the sense of isolation that was threatening to over-whelm me. But someone from the other side had spread the word, and not just to one television station but to all of them! I felt like a fool for following the rules.

The proctor opened the door to a room next to the grand jury chambers.

"This room is for the DA and police, but I guess it'll be all right for you to wait here."

Entering, I saw Marshall Slot and Jeff Strange, one of the assistant district attorneys, also waiting for things to begin. I wish I could have seen my face. It must have alternated be-tween blanched white and beet red. I'd gone from the media eye into a room with the Gestapo.

I had barely quieted my breathing when the door opened

again and Bart's former fiancée came in, looking as harried as I felt. My heart sank through the floor as I realized that she would also have to endure this. I was furious again, filled with impotent rage that someone would leak the news to the media and force both of us into this position.

"Oh, no! I'm so sorry you're here too," I told her. "I had no idea. Did you know about the news cameras before you came?"

"No, the police just told me I had to be here and that I couldn't tell anyone." She smiled wryly and said she was glad to see me too.

As the proctor closed the door, he told us we could stay but couldn't talk. So there we sat, like four strangers in a doctor's waiting room, trying with little success to ignore one another. I fought to control the swirling emotional storm I was feeling.

Within minutes Jeff left to help with the proceedings, and Marshall was called to testify. Bart's former fiancée and I sat in silence for a while, but before long we began visiting quietly, avoiding talk of anything associated with the shooting. She asked if I had noticed Adam Hipp, a friend and former classmate of Bart's, sitting on the bench, but I'd seen nothing but the glare of camera lights. Time dragged on.

After several hours, I was finally summoned to testify.

My first impressions were of a cluttered old room crammed with people, furniture, and boxes of documents. A water cooler and stacks of boxes partially blocked the pathway. I recognized Fred Felcman, the assistant district attorney who would be handling the prosecution. He was a stocky man with flowing white hair, a thick handlebar mustache, and expensive cowboy boots. A court reporter was wedged into the corner, and about twenty people crowded around a large old table. Fred rose, greeting me formally, and I was sworn in. There were no other introductions. It was all business. The questioning began.

"Mr. Whitaker, we are meeting today in a grand jury setting to get your testimony surrounding the events of December 10, 2003, including the murders of your wife, Tricia Whitaker, and son, Kevin Whitaker, and the disappearance of your son Bart Whitaker in June of 2004, and any other matters that might apply to this case. Will you please begin by telling us the events as you recall them of December 10, 2003."

I began to tell the story of that awful night, but Fred often interrupted and asked me to clarify details. We ventured onto many side topics: What was my net worth at the time of the shootings? (I told him.) What was the relationship like between Kevin and Bart? (Loving and caring from both directions.) Did I know that Bart was not in school at the time of the shootings? (No, and neither did Tricia.) Who suggested eating at Pappadeaux's restaurant? (Tricia called me on my way home from work, and we discussed it.) Were we expecting Bart to graduate the next week? (Yes.) Did we give him his graduation present that night? (Yes, an expensive watch.) Did we notice anything strange when we returned home? (Not at the time; later I realized no lights were on in the house.)

The interview went on and on, accompanied by the muffled clicking of the court reporter's machine as she took down everything. Fred asked questions about the incident when the Waco police alerted the Sugar Land police that Bart was coming home to kill us. I told him of our utter disbelief and that the Waco detective later concluded there was no basis for the charge other than a misunderstanding (heightened by alcohol) between roommates. Then Fred questioned me extensively about Bart's disappearance after the shooting. At some point we digressed to my decision to quit working for the construction company, and he requested details of my settlement agreement. For the first time I balked; I didn't see what that had to do with anything. I told them that those matters were private and that the legal agreement would not allow me to divulge any details, but one member of the jury continued to press. Finally the grand jury foreman decided that I did not have to disclose that information.

Throughout the session I did my best to answer honestly, but I often had to reply that I just couldn't remember details. The proceedings made me feel defensive, as if I were on trial, and that I had to justify my every action. Still smarting from the sting of betrayal at the presence of the news media, I asked if anyone within the district attorney's office had notified them; Fred replied that he had not.

After nearly two hours, the grand jury let me go. As I retreated to the waiting room, I lied when I told Bart's fiancée that it wasn't really that bad; privately I hoped that the cameras would follow me out and leave her alone. Marshall was back in the waiting area too, and he pointed out that I could walk forward faster than the camera guys could walk backward: if I headed straight toward them as fast as I could and stepped around them at the last moment, perhaps I could get outside unmolested.

I took a deep breath, opened the door, and stepped out

into the floodlights. Rushing forward, I noticed four camera crews now, but I made a beeline for the cameraman directly between me and the stairs. I rushed past him and sprinted down the stairs, two at a time. I felt like a NASCAR driver hitting clean air after fighting through the pack. Nearly free! The glass doors glowed with bright sunshine just ahead.

But the seconds it took to open them were all it took for the crews to catch up. I was surrounded again. More questions flew, and the cameras were in front of me as I tried to make my way to the street. I felt dirty, as if I were guilty of something, like a crooked official tracked down by *20/20*. I just wanted to get away!

"Please! I have no statement! Please! Just leave me alone!"

Brushing past them, I was surprised to realize that nearly everyone had honored my request and that I was almost free. Only one camera remained, but he stayed in front of me, no matter how swift my stride. All the way down one block and up another, he kept me locked in his lens. Turning the corner of the third block and seeing my truck, I remembered Marshall's suggestion and put on a burst of speed, bearing right down on him. Suddenly I realized that my face was inches from his lens and that he wasn't moving out of the away. Without thinking, I reached up, put my hand over the lens, and got around him, only to realize that I had just rewarded him with the kind of sensational footage he was looking for. My shoulders slumped, and I crawled into my truck feeling humiliated. He was still filming when I pulled away.

As I drove home I reflected on the terrible experience. It had left me feeling abused and ashamed. If such a thing were possible, I'd say this day was even more horrible than the night of the shooting except that the consequences weren't nearly as far-reaching. In the hospital that first night, I was still unaware that my son would become a suspect, and so I hadn't yet realized all the ways my loss would affect me. I only knew that something awful had happened, but I was surrounded by people who loved me, who were working for me and trying to make things better. I felt a sense of strength and community, of drawing together amid a raging storm with a commitment from each person that together we would prevail.

The ordeal I had just suffered was the exact opposite. With the exception of Bart's fiancée, who was under fire just as much as I was, I had been isolated from all support. Everyone there either had violated my privacy in return for television ratings, had lied to me about the session's secrecy, or was trying to put together an indictment charging my missing son with murder.

In retrospect, I realize this wasn't a fair assessment. The cynic in me recognizes that the news industry is driven by ratings, and the distinction between pure news and a form of mass entertainment has become blurred; but I also have to be honest with myself: the lurid details of this case made me fair game, and I should have expected the media to react to them.

I also realize that the district attorney and police were just doing their jobs of protecting society, trying to solve an awful crime, and they had volumes of details and information that were still hidden from me. All those boxes in the grand jury room probably weren't loaded with back issues of *Sports Illustrated*. I couldn't know then that some of the questions that struck me as odd really had purpose behind them. Then, all I knew was that the legal system seemed like the enemy.

Finally arriving home, I e-mailed my family and friends to warn them that I would be on TV that night.

Have you ever watched yourself on television? I hope you never have to. I sat stunned as I watched myself emerge from the stairs to be surprised by the media, and then rush from the courthouse. What a pathetic character, begging them to leave me alone! Every station in the country's fourth-largest city shared this with their viewers on the five, six, and ten o'clock news—including footage from the night of the shooting and of Bart's disappearance, and pictures of all of us. But the worst was the camera chase all the way to my truck. After making snide comments about Bart's running away under suspicious circumstances and the quality of our family, and as the camera showed me putting my hand over the lens, one anchor quipped, "Evidently Mr. Whitaker didn't want his picture taken." How witty and clever. He never pointed out that they got that shot three blocks from the courthouse. Guess that wasn't news.

I turned off the television and, realizing I was hungry, grabbed a banana. But as I chewed it, I was so upset by the day's experiences that I suffered my first bout of TMJ (a painful and potentially damaging displacement of the jaw due to stress) in twenty years. It was an accurate barometer of my emotional health. I will always bear scars from that horrible day.

Chapter 9

HURRICANES RITA
AND MARSHALL

A few quiet months would pass, and the constant stress in my heart from the grand jury settled down, as it had done after earlier shocks. But again it was a temporary lull. I should have felt the tension in the air as the next storm brewed.

My own private storm hit at 9:45 Friday evening, September 23, 2005. How ironic that Hurricane Rita would tear into the Texas gulf coast a few hours later.

Many people had feared that Rita would do to Houston what Katrina had done to New Orleans less than a month earlier, but that kind of destruction didn't materialize. Originally forecast as a category 4 or 5 hurricane, Rita diminished in strength and took a northerly turn just before landfall. Although it did severe damage to the Texas and Louisiana coasts, spawning hundreds of tornadoes and dumping huge amounts of water onto areas already devastated by Katrina, Houston itself was spared.

In fact, after I spent all day getting my home ready for Rita, the hurricane was almost a nonevent. Just before dark I took a walk around the neighborhood, noting all the homes whose windows were covered by sheets of plywood or crosshatched with duct tape. The neighborhood was nearly deserted, as most residents had joined two million other Houstonians fighting their way along paralyzed roads, trying to get out of town. As I walked, I was aware of the parallels between the storm and the legal system as I encountered it: moments of gusting winds were followed by dead calm, but things could change dramatically in a short time.

The sky was a strange shade of amber, as if I were looking at it through a sepia lens. I returned home under scattered raindrops and settled in to wait out what the weather reports were now projecting to be a quiet evening. It didn't turn out that way.

After eating supper, I decided to watch a movie. The prospect for dangerous winds and rain had vanished, and the predicted landfall was still three or four hours away. I chose *Reign of Fire*, a science fiction movie about the near future when the earth is taken over by dragons, starring a bald and tattooed Matthew McConaughey so bulked up as to be nearly unrecognizable.

I'll never forget when the phone call came. The biggest dragon of all had located a castle that surviving humans had converted into a shelter, and the beast was perched atop the walls, busy incinerating everything. I paused the action, picked up the phone, and was greeted by a voice I had come to dread.

"Hey, Kent, this is Marshall Slot. I wanted to let you know that Bart has been arrested. I can't tell you where he is, and it may take a day or two to get him back, but he's okay and should be in Sugar Land sometime this weekend. I wanted to give you a heads-up so you would know before the news story broke."

After I hung up, I sat frozen for several minutes, staring at the image of the dragon suspended in time and laying waste to everything. The call had done that to me. In the fifteen silent months since Bart had vanished, I had begun to hope that he really was innocent and that he had been able to start a new life somewhere else. I realize now that this was only wishful thinking, a defense mechanism to shield me from the horror of the situation. As long as he wasn't charged, or as long as the SLPD didn't give me some tangible reason for believing their theories, I could continue trying to put my life back together, hoping that Bart was safe. But beginning ten days earlier, with the arrest of Bart's friend and coworker Chris Brashear (who would later be charged as the shooter), this had become increasingly difficult. And with this one-minute phone call, everything changed.

Bart was in custody. He was being brought back to Fort Bend County to be charged with two murders.

The news hounds would be back on the hunt, again calling at five in the morning, looking for statements. He would go to trial, and I would finally hear the details of the police investigation and learn whether my son was responsible for the deaths of his mother and brother, my wife and child.

I turned off the television and sat in the dark, thinking. Other than notifying my family, I couldn't really do anything but pray for strength to get through it all. So as the outer edges of Hurricane Rita blew outside, I tried to turn it all over to God, and finally went to sleep.

The next morning's news coverage was limited to scenes of severe weather damage to the Beaumont area, with no mention of Bart. The police department wouldn't announce his arrest until he got back into town, so I had another day or two of quiet.

I phoned my parents and, without saying why, suggested we meet at their house after church on Sunday. There I told all of my family that Bart had been arrested and that the police planned to announce it publicly on Monday morning. I also called Tricia's family and Bart's former fiancée, leaving messages so they wouldn't be surprised by the news. As I drove away from my parents' home, Marshall called to say that Bart was already back in Sugar Land and that the department had decided to make the announcement that afternoon instead of waiting until Monday. He offered to let me see Bart for a few minutes before they spoke to the press. I was truly touched by this act of kindness and thanked him for his courtesy. I drove straight to the jail, but when I saw a news truck in the parking lot, I parked down the street at a restaurant instead. I called Marshall, and his partner Billy picked me up.

It was strange to see Bart again. I walked into a small visitation room where we were separated by thick, bulletproof glass. Sadness and shame filled his eyes, but he looked me directly in the eye and told me how sorry he was, that it was all his fault, and that he was going to do everything he could to make this as quick and painless for everyone as possible. This was the first time I realized that he might plead guilty. I gave up all doubt. I knew that he was responsible for my wife's and son's deaths.

As I recalled the many conversations Bart and I had shared in that first seven months, I relived the roiling emotions. I remembered the many two a.m. visits with God as I sat on our stairs, where I always went when sleep abandoned me. I was reminded of the many times I had identified with the father in the parable of the prodigal son and how I believed that God was using me to model his forgiveness and love. I told Bart I would stand with him through this.

Physically, he looked good. His hair was cut short, and he appeared tanned and healthy. I learned that he had been in Mexico and (ironically) had worked for a while as a bricklayer's helper for less than a dollar an hour, the same work he had done in our company a few summers earlier for more money. He also had worked in a furniture store and done odd jobs, and he had come to love the people there. Bart said that through deep introspection he had peeled back many layers of the onion that was his life and had returned to the young man he had been in seventh grade. He said the stranger wearing his clothes in 2003 no longer existed, and he never wanted to go back to that emotional and spiritual darkness. We didn't speak in specifics or depth about anything, even though Marshall had assured me that our meeting was private and would not be recorded or monitored, because I have watched too many movies to completely trust the police in situations like this. I wasn't taking any chances. We parted saying that we loved each other, and Bart telling me he was sorry for everything.

I went back into the hall, met Marshall, and exploded into tears. I couldn't stop the tidal wave of surging emotions: I was grateful that Bart was alive and healthy, that he had come to grips with what had happened, and that he had asked for forgiveness and claimed to have changed. Coupled with these feelings was the realization that for the first time he had essentially confessed to the murders of his mother and brother and that he had been lying to me for seven months about his innocence before running away, leaving me to clean up his mess. All of this loss was his fault, and there was no rational reason for any of it. What an incredible waste. If the case went to trial, no doubt I would receive more awful revelations as yet hidden from me.

Marshall had always claimed that the police had discovered horrible things in Bart's past—now it would all come out. I was ashamed of my doubt and negative thoughts about Marshall and the legal system while at the same time hating what their actions were doing to me, even as I held Bart responsible. Under the barrage of so many emotions, I was racked with grief and tears.

When I finally got myself under control, Marshall said he had called Matt Barnhill, and Matt was waiting to take me back to my car so I could avoid the media.

What a relief to see Matt and to know that I wasn't alone in this. He knew that I needed to talk, and we went to the Sonic drive-in so Matt could have one of his beloved Coke floats. As usual Matt helped me get some perspective. He pointed out that this day was bound to have come sometime and that now we were a step closer to finding the truth— and to Bart and me being able to rebuild our lives. I mentioned Bart's apparent spiritual growth and how he had intimated that he was going to confess. At the same time, we never lost sight of how he had deceived everyone before and might be trying to do it again. We must have visited at the drive-in for an hour, and I began to feel better. Matt dropped me off at my truck, and I drove home. Although I had expected to find news crews in the cul-de-sac, I saw only the neighborhood kids playing stickball.

That night I pondered many things, including the strange comment Bart had made about going back to the way he had been in seventh grade. What was happening then? How had it been different? For one thing, he was happy at school: he was making good grades, he liked his teachers, and they liked him. He was active in church and the youth group. At summer camp the year before, he had been one of the few attendees inducted into the camp's Honor of the Arrow for displaying a selfless attitude and concern for others.

He also was showing promise and earning accolades as a distance cyclist. Two years earlier he and I had begun riding our bicycles in organized two-day rides, and by the time he was finishing seventh grade, he'd gotten quite fast. We had ridden approximately four thousand miles together by then (which afforded us a lot of time to talk) and had upgraded from our heavy steel Schwinns to Trek 2300s, light carbon fiber road bikes. That spring and the next, Bart had been the fastest of more than a hundred riders thirteen years old and under to complete the ninety-eight-mile first day of the MS150, a grueling ride from Houston to Austin. So he was getting a lot of exercise (we trained year-round), feeling good about himself, doing well in school, and hanging out with a good crowd at church. I still didn't know what could have gone wrong in the following years that would lead to his arrest for murder. But it seemed that the reality of the shooting and his period of introspection in Mexico had been enough to restore him.

Everyone who visited Bart in jail noticed the difference. Before he ran away a year earlier, I had felt a vague sense that something wasn't right; but it was easy for all of us (our family, his fiancée and her family, and me) to chalk it up to the trauma of the shooting, and to believe that the police appeared to be going nowhere and were looking at Bart out of desperation. Of course, later we would learn just how much evidence they had. But at that time it seemed inconceivable that they were doing anything but grasping at straws.

When Bart was brought back from Mexico, much had changed. In the past, though he had never hoarded or taken things he didn't need and often was generous to others, Bart had always loved nice things. His closet was not overflowing, but what he did have was stylish and of high quality. He was conscious of his good looks and worked at being Mr. Cool. I recognized that touch of vanity in him, having felt similarly when I was younger. But I had always believed that, as it did with me, time and maturity would smooth out those rough edges.

Now it was as if Bart had matured decades in the short time he'd been gone. He no longer seemed prideful or even conscious of the good life and stylish things that had always been important to him. Oh, I guess he still recognized them; they just didn't matter anymore. He told me that living in the interior of Mexico had made him realize how trivial all of that was, since people concerned with keeping their family fed had little use for posing. (I would later recognize the significance of his term "posing.") He said he had come to realize that all he needed to make a living were a pair of jeans, work boots, and a T-shirt, and since all the people he had come to care for down there were poor, he too had grown content with having little.

I believe that some of this new maturity stemmed from realizing that for the first time in his life, he had accomplished living without help from anyone else. I think he was shocked to realize that he could have done this all along. Later, as I began to see behind the mask he had worn for years, I understood what a powerful lesson this must have been for someone who had no real sense of who he was inside and who believed he was incapable of living up to others' expectations without relying on deception.

I have been asked if this "reformed Bart" wasn't just

another of his personas spun to fool us. Of course that's possible, but I'm convinced that his actions and attitude prove otherwise. For the first time in his life, he wasn't making excuses for his behavior, and although the jail wouldn't allow it, he repeatedly asked for psychological help to determine why his mind had become so dark and confused. He seemed to genuinely want help, and he told me that he never wanted to go back to that mental hell. For a year and a half, from the day he was arrested until the trial began, he tried to confess but was kept from doing so upon advice of his attorneys, waiting in vain for the district attorney to back away from the death penalty. Bart displayed more concern for other people than in the past, and in a year and a half in county jail, he never once got into trouble. He exhibited calmness, peace, and a humility that had not been present before his flight to Mexico. All of us who knew him saw it.

If only the prosecutors could have seen these changes. To this day I believe that if they had, the fiasco would have ended within weeks of Bart's arrest: he could have pleaded guilty to a modified charge that spared his life and avoided a trial if only the prosecution could have spent time with him. But obstructions built into the legal system prevented this, and Bart's defense attorneys both claimed that if they gave the prosecution such access to their client, they could be disbarred.

Everybody played things so close to the vest. When I visited with Assisant District Attorney Fred Felcman for two hours just before the trial began, he told me that he still believed Bart had never shown any genuine regret or asked for forgiveness unless there was something to be gained. How could he think otherwise when all he saw was the Bart in the police files, the troubled young man who had existed three years earlier? If only he had been able to talk directly with Bart, I believe Mr. Felcman would have seen the changes too. But the only time they were ever in a room together was when they were standing before the judge in court.

Wedding bells!
Chapelwood United Methodist Church, June 21, 1975.

We still had a piece of that cake until the freezer broke in 2000.

FROM LEFT TO RIGHT: Happy times in our backyard with Bart, August 1980; Kent and Bart (eight months old) surrounded by toys at the Conroe lake house, August 1980; a mother's quiet love— Tricia and Bart, summer 1980.

LEFT: Bart and me on a training ride, spring 2000. If you added the lengths of all our rides together, they would stretch two-thirds of the way around the world. RIGHT: Bart, heading for Baylor University, August 1998.

LEFT TO RIGHT, TOP TO BOTTOM: Kevin (six months old) with "Papa," Tricia's dad—these two were very close, and Kevin idolized him; Kevin (two years old) at Galveston beach; team captain Kevin with the first place team trophy from the 1995 JCC citywide tournment; Kevin hits a stand-up double in the 1998 fall baseball league; all three of us guys were terrors on a Jet Ski-- here Kevin makes a 90-degree turn at 60 mph; high school graduation, May 2002. (Honor cords? Who needs them! Kevin did not earn an honor society rope, so he made up for it with this white extension cord.)

LEFT: Bart was always happy as a child, and
very proud of being a big brother, August 1984.
RIGHT: Bart and Kevin, fall 1986. Kevin loved climbing things.

Easter Sunday, 1986, in front of our house.

Kevin (fifteen years old) and Bart (nineteen) on a tour
of New York City with Tricia and her mom, March 1999.

Sunset at Cancún, summer of 2002.

Bart (twenty-two years old), Tricia, and Kevin (eighteen)
in front of our house, Christmas 2002.

Tricia and me, cruising Lake Conroe, summer 2000.
Photo courtesy of Captain Kevin

Bart and Kevin with me mountain biking in Colorado
as we celebrated my fifty-fifth birthday, July 2003.

December 10, 2003. About to leave for the restaurant.
I see a sadness, a trapped look of resignation, in Bart's eyes.
Kevin (like the rest of us) had no idea what was coming.

Leaving the restaurant. By now I believe Bart was on emotional autopilot.
How tragic that his self-hatred had gone unchecked and unnoticed.
Kevin and Tricia would be murdered within thirty minutes.

Chapter 10

SWITCHING HORSES

Now that Bart had been arrested and was back in Sugar Land awaiting indictment, things started moving, and Dan began developing legal strategies. Bart told him the same thing he had told me in my first visit to the jail: he was willing to plead guilty to spare me and Tricia's family from having to endure a trial. The only problem was that the district attorney was still going for the death penalty, and as long as that was a possibility, Dan wouldn't let Bart confess. Since trials consist of two parts (the guilt/innocence phase and the punishment phase), if Bart confessed, the trial would go immediately into the punishment phase (which meant either life in prison or death). Bart was ready to accept spending his natural life in prison, but if he confessed without having the death penalty taken off the table, Dan said that it would seriously limit his legal options in the punishment phase, making it more likely that the death penalty would result.

Dan was confident that a deal could be struck, since even in Texas (which is famous for its executions), many district attorneys were starting to back away from the death penalty. Public sentiment across the country was turning away from it as well, and Texas juries were becoming less inclined to grant executions.

Texas has two types of capital murder conviction: Capital Murder, Life in Prison; and Capital Murder, Death Penalty. When compared with pursuing a conviction for Capital Murder, Life in Prison, the cost and time involved to go after a death penalty conviction were enormous. For one thing, the jury selection process was much more involved, giving the defense greater advantages. And since only a unanimous decision secures a death penalty, the prosecutor "loses" if even one of the twelve jurors holds out for life in prison.

Dan reasoned that in light of those odds and the fact that all the surviving victims (my family and Tricia's) had pleaded that execution not be pursued, the death penalty would probably be eliminated as a potential punishment. (While the request of the victim's family to abandon the death penalty is not binding on the prosecution, it is significant: such pleas are seldom ignored. In this case *both sides* of the victims' family campaigned strongly against it.)

I had a lot of confidence in Dan because I had known him for years. In fact, it was only because of that connection that I had consulted him in the first place. Back in early 2004, when Bart began looking for an attorney, it was more as a contingency plan than something we expected to need. If I had not known Dan for so long, we probably would have started with someone less high profile. At that time (a month after the shooting) all I knew was that the police considered Bart a suspect. Although I believed it was just a matter of time before they moved on, I couldn't take the risk of being unprepared. I needed to secure legal counsel—just in case.

Choosing a lawyer is a little like choosing a new barber: you don't know you've made a mistake until it's too late. You do your homework, but in the end you must step out in faith, hoping you got the right one.

Hair grows back, but the effects of bad legal decisions are permanent.

I knew a lot of lawyers, but capital murder defense is rarified air, and the sort of discipline you never expect to need. Until circumstances throw you into that arena, you tend to think of attorneys as hired gunslingers. But your perspective changes when you need one, because when you do, it isn't like choosing between generic and brand-name cinnamon. Suddenly you not only want a gunslinger, you want the baddest dude in Dodge.

Fortunately, I knew one of the very best. I first met Dan Cogdell when he was in middle school. Tricia's younger brother had grown up with him, and Dan was a fixture at their home, riding up on increasingly larger motorcycles as the years went by. I'd watched him graduate from high school, go into law, and become the protégé of world-famous defense lawyer Richard "Racehorse" Haynes, a Texas legal legend if there ever was one. After being mentored for six years under that icon, Dan struck out on his own, quickly making a name for himself. He had successfully defended many high-profile clients, including a former Branch Dividian in the Waco assault, an alleged ranch-slave torturer, an unorthodox cancer doctor, and an Enron employee implicated in a high-profile Nigerian finance scheme. Dan was the sort of legal rock star you would want if someone in your family were charged with a serious crime. I called him in mid-January.

After meeting with Bart and me for nearly two hours, Dan agreed to represent Bart, but he felt that nothing would come of the investigation. He had known Bart since my son was a baby and was aware of how inexperienced the Sugar Land Police Department was in dealing with murder. Our case was the first murder ever handled by the lead detective. Once the SLPD got some traction, Dan felt the case would take off in an entirely different direction. His first move was to hire an investigator to gather information on the man who had committed suicide the evening of the shooting and on the girl and her boyfriend. Perhaps we could learn something that would change the police department's thinking.

What I didn't know was that before our meeting, Dan had called Tricia's brother to get his thoughts on the matter. Dan told him that he could always get clients but that lifelong friends were rare, and he would suggest alternative counsel if Tricia's brother had reservations. To the contrary, her brother was enthusiastic and told Dan that he would be glad to have him involved.

Time passed slowly during the early months of 2004, but as far as we could tell, nothing was happening in the investigation. I would receive occasional calls from the police with vague and disturbing insinuations, but never anything illuminating; they shared no details and made no specific charges. It seemed the only purpose of the calls was to frighten me. After Bart fled to Mexico, Dan occasionally checked in with the police, but until they offered some information, there was little for him to do—which was fine with me.

Then, in mid-September 2005, the Sugar Land Police Department announced that three warrants were being issued in the case: Chris Brashear would be charged as the trigger man, and Steven Champagne, another of Bart's friends and coworkers, as the escape driver. The third person had not yet been named, but speculation was high that Bart would be charged with planning the murders. Less than two weeks later, Bart was arrested.

Dan then began an elaborate dance with the DA's office, sounding them out on whether they would accept a plea bargain. He'd had some previous dealings with Fred Felcman, the assistant district attorney who would be handling the case, and felt that Fred was a straight-up guy who spoke his own mind and would honestly consider our arguments. Early results seemed hopeful, with the prosecutors offering encouragement, and Dan felt it was only a matter of time before an agreement was reached. In return for dropping the death penalty, we offered a guilty plea with stacked sentences (meaning that the second forty-year sentence would not begin until the first was completed, effectively ensuring that Bart would never leave prison). This dance would last a long time, with the prosecution always a concern or two away from accepting Bart's confession.

We tried to meet every one of their requests. Early in the discussions, Fred told Dan that he needed to receive a proffer from Bart. This is a document that isn't admissible in court but outlines a person's involvement in a crime, including names and details. It's a major good-faith move because it answers unresolved questions for the prosecution. In essence, the defense shows all their cards. When Dan explained this to us, Bart assumed that this was his responsibility, and eagerly wrote a long and detailed letter confessing his guilt and expressing how sorry he was.

Apparently, Bart misunderstood who was to write the proffer because his letter was never given to Fred. Instead, one of Dan's associates wrote it, and when it was sent to the DA's office, they thought that Bart had written it. Fred later told me that he was incensed at what he perceived as the letter's cold legalism and lack of remorse. I believe he thought that Dan was trying to "outlawyer" and intimidate him and that Dan's first goal was to get the state to back away from the death penalty, then whittle away the number of years until few were left. It was all wrong and a terrible misunderstanding, but a long time passed before Fred learned that Bart had not written the proffer. By then the DA's office had undergone a change of heart and was no longer considering a plea bargain. The DA never saw the proffer Bart had written, and he claimed in the trial that Bart had never shown remorse.

At the time I believed that the DA's actions were partly

political because he was engaged in an active primary race, with the general election to follow six months later. Fort Bend County is politically conservative, and the murders were the biggest crime news in recent history. Although the county was maturing, the political leadership still operated with the good-old-boy mentality that had been in place for a long time.

Death penalty decisions are not made in a vacuum. Even though it might make good economic and strategic sense to strike a deal (given that the county could spend several hundred thousand dollars to try a death penalty case in court, and knowing that they had a guilty plea just waiting for them to accept), the DA probably still felt that he couldn't afford to appear lenient on such an emotionally charged crime in an election year. It could even be argued that if he declined to pursue the death penalty in the case of a rich white boy who had killed his mom and brother, it would be difficult to seek the death penalty should a poor black boy be charged in some future murder case.

Since Bart would be charged with two deaths, the DA could reasonably claim that the crime deserved the death penalty. No argument there, but just because the crime qualifies for the ultimate punishment doesn't mean it's mandatory or even the right thing to do. Besides, Texas has a law that other states don't have, which makes everyone involved in a crime equally responsible. Even though they did not pull the trigger that resulted in the two deaths, Bart and the driver could be sentenced to death as easily as the actual shooter.

Seeking the death penalty in Bart's case was curious, however, in light of the DA's decision (already announced) not to pursue the death penalty against Chris Brashear, the alleged shooter.

I believe that many factors played a role in their decision to pursue the death penalty, including a basic philosophy of how crime should be punished. People with different personality types naturally gravitate toward different professions. By the time they graduate from high school, most kids have taken a personality profile to help them make career or collegiate decisions. For example, if someone is quiet and shy, it might make better sense to pursue a career in research or library science than to go into commodity futures trading or used-car sales. While results of such tests are imperfect and exceptions exist, they are useful because they indicate strong trends that apply in most cases. I believe it takes a specific set of characteristics to sustain a successful career as an assistant district attorney and that those characteristics predispose a person to make the choice to pursue the death penalty in a case like Bart's.

To become a district attorney, one must already be an attorney, and profiles show that most lawyers are smarter than the average person, are aware of it and proud of it, and even keep an internal score on how they're doing in comparison with other attorneys. Trial lawyers tend to be aggressive by nature: they argue for a living. Conflict is not necessarily something to be avoided, and since their place on the status ladder is determined by their effectiveness in the courtroom, the win/loss ratio is important. Friends in the profession have told me that sometimes winning becomes everything, and justice suffers.

But not every lawyer would make a good assistant district attorney: it takes a special subset of personality traits to make a good DA, especially one who chooses to make that his or her career rather than using it as a stepping-stone to something else.

Many young attorneys spend time as assistant prosecutors because it's a good way to learn the ropes, and it can lead, in a few years, to a more lucrative career as a defense attorney. Some remain in the prosecutor's office with political aspirations, others because they're not good enough to succeed elsewhere. But the latter definitely was not the case with Fred— he is an excellent lawyer: quick of wit, analytical, prepared, and aggressive. Those like Fred who choose to remain in the DA's office likely do so because they love what they do more than they desire the larger paychecks a private practice would bring. Some of their compensation is in the form of satisfaction: knowing that they're protecting society from the scum of the universe, much as Will Smith's character did in the *Men in Black* movies. My guess is that their worldview has very few shades of gray. And there's probably a strong brotherhood between their ranks and those in the police department, because the two groups seem to share some personality traits, a common worldview, and a common cause: to put away the bad guys. The popular television series *Law and Order* is a great example of how these two groups often are in sync in their attitudes about crime.

The Fort Bend District Attorney's Office (and Fred Felcman in particular) probably felt a visceral repulsion to what Bart had done and believed that putting him to death was the only way to protect society (including the society within prison) from a man who could commit such a horrible crime. In many ways society is safer because of district attorneys like Fred, who really do provide the critically important service of putting criminals behind bars.

I know that the world is not a perfect place, and decisions rarely involve only a single issue—especially when powerful political components exist, as in this case. Arguments pro and con must be weighed. And while I was not privy to their discussions and cannot therefore know the reasoning behind their decision, in the end the DA's office did choose to pursue the death penalty.

From my perspective, it is a shame that they ignored the compromise that would have allowed Bart to plead guilty and accept two stacked capital murder sentences. That would have saved the county several hundred thousand dollars by avoiding the expense of a capital murder trial; saved the state of Texas the enormous expense of defending the automatic federal and state appeals that must follow a guilty verdict; cleared up the local court docket for more than two months; put Bart in prison without parole or time off for good behavior until at least his 106th birthday; honored the victims' families' repeated and passionate pleas not to pursue the death penalty; and saved me, my family, and Tricia's family from the terrible emotional ordeal and scarring of a trial. Not to mention the huge savings in legal expenses for me if a trial had been avoided. I just couldn't see what the DA's office gained that justified what it cost both families.

My flaw was my naïveté: I could not understand why what

seemed reasonable to me might not be reasonable to someone else. Fred, looking at the situation through his worldview, no doubt had the same confusion about me.

Whatever their reasoning, the prosecutors chose to reject the plea bargain. But even before it became apparent that they would pass on a deal, a new and unexpected complication was brewing.

Occasional conflict had always existed between Tricia's family and me. I guess that's to be expected when an in-law works in a family business, as I had done for thirty years. I'd never placed too much emphasis on these disagreements; every business setting has some discord, but her brother and I were friends, worked well together, and were very good at our different responsibilities. The company was successful, and making money goes a long way toward keeping the peace.

When it became clear in the fall of 2004 that I would leave the construction company, however, some of that friction flared up. I think part of the tension was that Tricia's family had come to the conclusion that Bart was responsible for the murders and didn't like the idea that I was trying to defend him. So when Bart was arrested and talk of a trial began, Tricia's brother began to rethink his approval of his friend Dan's involvement and decided that he didn't want him to participate any longer. He told Dan that their friendship would suffer if he stayed on, and that he needed to drop Bart, leaving the defense to someone else. Dan tried to explain that since he had accepted my retainer, he had an obligation as well as the desire to see the case through, but Tricia's brother was persistent. Dan asked me if I would release him from our agreement.

I was dumbfounded. I couldn't believe that Dan would consider such a thing. I told Dan that I appreciated his dilemma but I wasn't going to make it easy for him. Bart was still his client, and if anybody was going to release Dan, it would have to be Bart. When I asked why the family had changed their minds, Dan replied that they were worried that his legal skills were good enough to get Bart off on some technicality— and they didn't want Bart ever to get back out on the street, where he could possibly hurt their family again. Understandable, but at this point Dan had already given the DA a proffer outlining Bart's involvement in the shooting; Bart would never get out of jail, whether he received the death penalty or not. All this request did was to distract Dan's attention from defense strategy as he wrestled with the problem of trying to fulfill his obligation and still keep his lifelong friend. Dan knew he needed to make a decision, and that both choices were bad. The DA's office quickly picked up on the undertones of discord as well.

We reached a point in the spring of 2006 when two things became obvious: First, in my judgment, the DA was showing signs of having dealt in bad faith and was giving no indication that he would accept our deal for life in prison with stacked forty-year sentences, even after receiving a written proffer. Second, Dan was still struggling with how to stay on board without damaging his friendship with Tricia's brother. This meant that the only way to move forward was to shake up the attorney mix.

Dan and I came up with a plan. To avoid a trial, we needed to apply pressure on the DA's office; and to do that we needed to show them that we were still unified. We reasoned that my brother-in-law's major objection to Dan's involvement was his belief that Dan was good enough to get Bart acquitted. If we added another attorney to the team whose responsibility would be to handle the trial, it would free Dan to concentrate on making a deal. Presumably, this would soothe the family's objections, since Dan wouldn't be arguing the case. Dan wanted to stay active in the case because he feared that the DA might never have been serious about reaching a compromise.

Assistant DA Fred Felcman seemed eager and pleased to think that Dan might be quitting the case, even to the point of asking him to confirm that he was doing so, which irritated Dan to no end. Dan felt that it would put pressure on the DA's office when they heard that he was actually staying and gearing up for a fight by hiring additional help.

With Dan's assistance I interviewed three attorneys and decided on Randy McDonald. Randy was a veteran of two dozen capital murder cases and had achieved much success. Perhaps ten years older than Dan, he was as quiet and methodical as Dan was gregarious and spontaneous. With either of them good enough to get the job done on his own, they would make a formidable team. Dan was larger than life, and if you weren't careful, you could be dazzled by his flair and reputation, overlooking his keen mind and eloquent arguments. Randy never forgot anything and would lay a series of traps that you never saw until it was too late. One attorney would blind you with his rock-star flash, and the other with his understated Matlock persona.

Our interview had quickly revealed Randy's intelligence and insight: he quietly suggested possible tactics that were simple but clever. He understood that my goal was not acquittal: we all knew that was never going to happen. All I wanted was to spare Bart's life and keep his options open so that he could serve God in prison, should he choose that path. While I was encouraged by Randy's grasp of courtroom maneuvers, he was more cerebral than Dan, telling us that perhaps his strongest suit was his skill in jury selection. Maybe when they learned that Randy had joined the team, the prosecution could be moved to accept our proposal.

But as we soon learned, that wouldn't happen; the DA had dug in his heels, and a deal would not be forthcoming, regardless of who was on the defense team. Dan was right back in his old dilemma, and I felt sorry for him. Fearing that we might lose the solidarity of Tricia's family in the question of life versus death (which would be important in the penalty phase of the trial), and with our growing faith in Randy's abilities, I told Bart that I thought it best to release Dan from his commitment. Bart had independently come to the same conclusion, so with his blessing we made the transition. We had entered the Randy McDonald era.

Not long after Randy took the reins, a court hearing was held in which both sides were to set mutually agreeable ground rules. Randy hoped that he could still engineer a plea deal but knew that the only way this could be accomplished was to make the death penalty more trouble than it was worth. Consequently, he successfully argued for several legal hindrances that the prosecution had not expected. This put them on notice that he would contest every move, and while I think it frustrated the district attorney, in the end it was ineffective. We had reached the point that sometimes happens in negotiations where one party becomes intractable, and the only solution is to see the fight through to its bitter end.

During the months leading up to the trial, Randy spent many hours talking with Bart and me. An astute observer of humanity, he recognized early that Bart tried to keep others from seeing what was really going on inside him and that he was good at analyzing people and playing to their expectations.

The first time Randy told Bart to stop it, describing exactly what Bart was doing and what Bart was expecting Randy to do next, a shocked look crossed Bart's face. No one but Tricia or I had ever done that before. It was the beginning of a tremendous breakthrough. Over the course of a month, as Randy did this several times, Bart came to realize that he couldn't fool Randy.

I believe this was the third part in a four-step approach God used to break through Bart's titanium shell. He had begun the campaign to regain Bart's heart through my initial forgiveness and acceptance, which confused and amazed my son as he tried to grasp that reality. The second component had been the seven months of intense lessons in God's Word that Bart and I shared as we studied the grace and forgiveness God extends to everyone who is repentant. This is incredibly attractive to those who suffer guilt; if they can ever grasp both their need and the reality that God has forgiven them, they can sometimes forgive themselves too. In Mexico Bart took this promise and my actions and digested them. He took a closer look at his life and realized how a series of many tiny steps had led to this tragedy. He came to the conclusion that he did not want to remain as he had become. In this third step, Bart realized that he wouldn't be able to hide behind his mask any longer now that Randy had seen through it. The fourth, and most important step, would soon follow.

By the time Bart was captured and returned to Sugar Land, he had already made great strides, and I continued to show the unconditional forgiveness that God allowed me to feel for him. A case in point was a letter I sent him in January 2006, six months after his arrest. I had been telling him I had forgiven him for everything, but I wanted him to understand what that "everything" meant. In three typewritten pages I listed some of what the events of December 10 had cost me: My best friend, lover, and wife was gone forever. I had lost both of my boys and would never have daughters-in-law or grandchildren to love. I would never see my sons graduate from college or get their first job promotion. Family vacations were a thing of the past.

I'd suffered obvious physical losses as well. I could no longer reach much of my back because the damage of the gunshot wound reduced my arm's range of motion. My mental recall was badly affected as a result of post-traumatic stress disorder. An ever-present sense of loss and sadness and barrenness simmered just below the surface, keeping me from potential romantic relationships. There were other losses as well, some of which were less obvious. Tricia had been the family historian, and with her gone, I no longer remembered people, events, and details. I had no one left to ask about them. Entire chapters of my life were now lost forever, and I didn't even know what it was that was lost.

Financially the experience had been devastating. I took a loss in selling Bart's home, and the mounting legal fees were staggering. I was out of a job. My company-paid medical and vehicle allowances were gone.

I ended the letter pointing out that all of these losses (and more) were real and that I wasn't responsible for any of it—they were the result of the murders he had arranged. Then I reminded him that I had forgiven everyone involved in all of it. I told him to go back and reread the letter, one line at a time, imagining all of the ramifications that particular loss had brought into my life and the lives of others. Then I told him to hear me say, "My son, I love you! All is forgiven!" and not to move to the next line and loss until he could believe that my forgiveness was real. When he finally got to the end of the list, having accepted my forgiveness for all of it, I suggested that he pray a prayer of thanksgiving, remembering that we all make serious mistakes, and while some are more serious than others, God doesn't check the sin Richter scale; he forgives everything, and so have I.

Through this exercise Bart was reassured that my forgiveness was real—and that it was merely a shadow of what God was offering him. When Randy showed Bart that it was no longer possible to fake his way through life, the third phase of God's plan to reach my son was complete. Bart was finally ready to take a terrifying leap of faith. Knowing that he had an anchor in his father and that God's promises offered the assurance of even greater strength through the Holy Spirit, he took hesitant steps to let Randy and me see what was inside, trembling toward that fourth and final stage. With halting fingers, Bart loosened the knots that for years had kept the mask in place, hiding the horror behind it. He did what Absalom couldn't do. He made the decision to let in the light.

He wrote me a letter.

Chapter 11

BEHIND THE MASK

I n July 2006, two and a half years after the murders, I received a wrenching, three-page letter from Bart that whispered clues to what might have led to our family tragedy. I already knew *what* had happened; the mystery that haunted me was, why? Without that insight, how could I know if Bart was still the same person he had been on the night of the shooting or if the changes in my son could be real?

His words broke my heart, but at least I could begin to understand. Here are some excerpts from that letter.

> *I have been reading the Bible a lot today . . . and that
> got me to thinking a lot about my faith. I realize that I*

*am a pretty crappy Christian, especially for someone in my
position. I don't pray like I should, when I do I am easily
distracted, sometimes realizing that I had been praying
but couldn't remember if I finished or not. I forget to pray
for people when I tell them I am going to. . . . I know that
there is more to [a relationship with God] than [asking for
things], and I can tell someone a lot about being a Christian
and [about] God, but internally the talk and the walk are
light-years apart. The Bible says "God is love," but I don't
really know what that means. . . .*

*I felt love for my fiancée, but [also a] relief that at least
with her I had an identity, some mold to conform to, which
eliminated a lot of confusion. Is that love? I say I love you,
but what I really feel is mainly respect for the man you are.
I loved Mom and Kevin, but I also felt a lot of hatred, and I
have no idea why. I think I really don't know what anything
feels like. I have all these descriptions of words like "hate"
or "envy," but I don't know that what I feel fits into any of
them or if I really feel anything at all. I think I made myself
try to feel certain ways because that is what other people do
in these situations. Is a reflection of an emotion real? I don't
know. I don't really know much of anything except for this
place, my existence, is not real life. It's some sort of half-life,
where I am a bad copy, a rippled reflection of what a human
being should be. I have all the external characteristics of
being a man, but under the skin I cannot identify anything.
You once congratulated me for taking off the masks. I
understand now that the masks were not primarily a tool*

of deception but rather an attempt to become something, anything. . . .

I wish I had lived different, Dad. I wish I could have made you proud. I wish I had done something other than "take" all the time from everyone. I am sorry for the lives I ruined and sorrier yet that there isn't really anything I can do to rectify any of it anymore. Most of all, I am sorry that I have no real reason for any of this mess. I am not the person I was in 2003. I don't know what any of this means. . . .

I have always been very confused about everything, and I attempted to cover this up with certainty and bluster. I never seemed to make any dent into the big hole inside of me. I could never seem to fill it, when everyone else seemed bursting with life. I think I wanted revenge for being born.

I hadn't realized how different Bart's world was from the rest of the family's. He lived his life in a reality that had became more and more removed from ours. But the events of December 10, 2003, caused an emotional Hiroshima that eventually led him back to God and restoration with me. That night was a dividing line that separated the part of his life in which he was getting worse from the new life that would make him better. Positive forces began influencing his life; the letter was evidence of those changes and that his road to healing had begun.

About two months after Bart fled to Mexico, I went for a walk through the neighborhood. It was cool for August, and many people were taking advantage of the lovely evening. I came across two women I knew and ended up walking with them and chatting. The conversation eventually got around to Bart and his disappearance. One of them asked me how I was holding up.

"To be honest, it's really hard. But our relationship since the shootings has been good. He and I spent a lot of time just talking about things. Being under suspicion, he needed to know that I will always be in his corner."

"You remind me of Job," she replied.

I chuckled. "You aren't kidding! But you know who I feel more like? That father in the story of the prodigal son. I've tried to pattern my life after that guy. He was abandoned too, but he continued to pray for his missing son, just as I'm doing, always hoping that he would return. And one day he did. The good thing is that Bart and I had seven months together before he left. I worked hard to show that my love was unconditional, and we talked in-depth about forgiveness and grace. He has the answers if he'll just listen to them."

Later that night I thought more about that parable and realized that the brokenhearted father's patience and the love he felt for his son—even though he knew the boy's decisions were ruining his young life—were but a shadow of the far deeper love God has for us.

After Bart was brought back to Texas, he told me that God had used me to reach him. Bart had been listening during those seven months of discipleship, and in Mexico he made the connection: he could trust God the Father once again because he had learned to trust me.

While Bart had made the decision to pursue a relationship

with the Lord, he was inexperienced with drawing on that source of strength, and he was still in a life-or-death battle with his inner fears. He finally faced them by writing the letter, and for the first time he revealed the mental nightmares he lived with every day.

I wrestled with making sense of those nightmares for a long time. I had been told that he would not be able to receive psychiatric help while in jail, but he was my son and I needed to understand. I was not trained in psychoanalysis so I knew that trying to figure out whatever mental illness brought Bart to December 10 would put me in waters way over my head. With input from a lot of people, Bart and I have worked hard to figure this out. Eventually the pieces of the puzzle started coming together and I began to understand the problem: a "real" Bart didn't even exist. He didn't have a sense of who he was because nothing inside him was real. He explained it this way: other people had an inner core that was their essence (and which they not only built their personality and lives upon but also retreated to in times of stress); Bart was empty. He had only a visual exterior, with no supporting foundation, framework, or substance. Such emptiness required him to improvise responses based on the conditions he encountered and whom he was with instead of making decisions based on who he was inside.

For years Bart had tried unsuccessfully to fill that emptiness by doing what he thought a normal person should do and by being what he thought people wanted him to be, hoping that eventually something would permanently graft to his soul. He wanted to become a real person, but every time he looked for internal direction, the cupboard was bare. This emptiness produced a deep shame, for in his eyes these problems devalued him as a person. He tried to hide it by pretending to be normal, wearing one mask when he was with us, a slightly different one when he was with his girlfriend, another at work, and yet another at school. They were all lies. In his early teens he finally grew exhausted from trying and gave up on ever having a real self to guide his actions. Thus he opened the doors to the tragedy that was to come.

How different things might have been if Tricia and I had known and been able to help fight what was happening inside the son we loved.

Bart told me that he vividly remembered when the confusion over his identity and belief system took their fatal turn. On Christmas Eve, when he was in eighth grade, we were coming home from a candlelight service after visiting my parents. Riding in the dark that evening, he recalled a poem he had read recently—William Blake's "The Little Boy Lost":

> "Father, father, where are you going?
> O do not walk so fast.
> Speak father, speak to your little boy,
> Or else I shall be lost."

> The night was dark, no father was there,
> The child was wet with dew.
> The mire was deep, & the child did weep,
> And away the vapour flew.

I'm lost too, he thought to himself as he looked at the back of my head, *and you don't even know it. I hate this! God, where are you when I need you so bad?*

You call yourself God, but you aren't God. If you were, why do you let all these things happen? I've tried for years to do what's right, but what has it gotten me? Nothing! I wouldn't cheat on the history test and got a C, but Mark and Jimmy cheated and got A's. The girls in Miss Johnson's class laughed at me when I tried to stick up for that weird new kid. Wasn't that what you wanted me to do? I hate how you never answer my prayers. I don't think you even care. I don't think you give a flip about me or anybody. Who needs you! What good is it to try and try and try and always fail? Why can't I be confident like that jerk Randy—why do you always make me feel so empty? Why can't I be happy? You're the dad in the poem, aren't you? You take us out into the lonely darkness and disappear, leaving us all alone. If this is how you treat people who try to do what you want, I don't want or need you anymore! I just don't believe in you.

Bart said he began to shake when he admitted to himself the resentment and anger that had been building in secret for so long. Like the prodigal son, he made the free-will decision to reject his faith. Not only was he without an inner core of strength to rely on, but he also had renounced the value system that he had trusted. Life was completely empty.

How sadly strange that the rest of us in the car were warm and happy, anticipating the sharing of gifts to come in the morning, while Bart sat in the darkness, feeling cut off from the rest of the world and taking those first blind steps that he did not realize would eventually bring him to the tragedy of December 10.

Abandoning both his faith and the hope of ever being whole had profound negative effects. Though Bart continued to be outwardly charming and social, inside resided a deep sense of failure: he believed he had shamed his parents—we just didn't know it yet. He was torn between two horrible choices: without help to find who he really was, he was convinced he would fail in his desperate attempt and desire to make us proud; but he also was convinced that if he revealed his need and we learned the truth, we would be as disgusted with him as he had become with himself. He saw no way out.

Bart was devoid of honest self-esteem: how could self-esteem exist when *self* did not exist? He wore a false mask of confidence and bravado that was the framework upon which all of his other masks were based. He loathed the truth that he didn't have the courage to face his imperfections or ask for help; he knew he was a coward. The mere act of facing himself each day became increasingly unbearable. To numb himself from these truths, his subconscious created a thickening crust of detachment to hide his loathing so that he could function. Though this crust got thicker, nothing really changed.

He did a remarkably good job of masking these horrible truths; survival meant keeping his family in the dark. He thought he had to fool us, or we would reject him. As time passed, these destructive coping mechanisms fed off of one another, growing stronger and stronger. Bart became less connected to reality and formulated ways to escape the life in which he felt trapped. Surely another life would be better. Any other life.

At some point, in high school, he began adopting what he

saw as cool, dangerous guy's traits—a sort of combination of James Bond and Bruce Willis. Bart embraced the role of the glib man outside society looking in: the tough guy who ignored the rules, always smart enough to avoid getting caught. It turned out that he already had been introduced to a fictional character that seemed to be everything he wanted to be.

Jim diGriz, the main character in the sci-fi novel *The Adventures of the Stainless Steel Rat* (Harry Harrison, 1978), reflected on his sense of separation from the world:

> It was a nice ride to the spaceport . . . and I had time to gather my thoughts. Even time to be a little philosophical.
>
> My life is so different from that of the overwhelming majority of people in our society that I doubt if I could even explain it to them. They exist in a fat, rich union of worlds that have almost forgotten the meaning of the word crime. There are few malcontents and even fewer that are socially maladjusted. The few of these that are born, in spite of centuries of genetic control, are caught early and the aberration quickly adjusted.
>
> That is almost the full extent of crime in our organized, dandified society. Ninety-nine percent of it, let's say. That one percent is me, and a handful of men scattered around the galaxy. Theoretically we can't exist, and if we do exist we can't operate—but we do. We are the rats in the wainscoting of society—we operate outside of their barriers and outside of their rules. Society had more rats when the rules were

looser, just as the old wooden buildings had more rats than the concrete buildings that came later. But they still had rats. Now that society is all ferroconcrete and stainless steel there are fewer gaps between the joints, and it takes a smart rat to find them. A stainless steel rat is right at home in this environment.

It is a proud and lonely thing to be a stainless steel rat—and it is the greatest experience in the galaxy if you can get away with it. The sociological experts can't seem to agree why we exist, some even doubt that we do.

A few years back I wrote a small book on the subject that was rather well received. My theory is that the aberration is a philosophical one, not a psychological one. At a certain stage the realization strikes through that one must either live outside of society's bonds or die of absolute boredom. There is no future or freedom in the circumscribed life and the only other life is complete rejection of the rules. There is no longer room for the soldier of fortune or the gentleman adventurer who can live both within and outside society. Today it is all or nothing. To save my own sanity I chose the nothing.

I think Bart saw himself as a stainless steel rat.

The humorous sci-fi Rat novels made for spirited entertainment for readers like Bart and me. We respected such characters—not for their moral shortcomings but for their ability to outwit adversaries rather than rely on brute strength.

The books always ended with Jim diGriz, aka the Stainless Steel Rat, doing the right thing when it counted. While I enjoyed reading about the Rat's adventures and admired his mental agility, I never considered him a role model. But Bart tried on the persona of the Stainless Steel Rat. Probably part of the attraction was that Bart could almost fool himself into thinking that, like the Rat, his actions would ultimately be for good.

Bart was a good enough liar to play this game of deception without apparent consequences, except for the high school break-in. People often believe an outright fabrication if it is spoken with conviction, and the awful truth was that Bart was smart enough and engaging enough that he could usually pull it off. Like the Rat, Bart despised those who weren't his perceived mental equals, including Tricia and me. He saw us as weak because over the years, when conflicts arose, she and I often allowed others to have their way rather than oppose them, taking into consideration factors other than just who won. Bart hated our "weakness," and he had drifted far enough from reality to entertain the irrational thought that he might not even be our son, since we were such disappointingly average people, and he was far superior.

Gardens must receive vigilant care, or weeds will soon dominate, choking out the good things that once flourished. The same is true of the mind, and Bart was sinking ever deeper into his mental briar patch. He graduated from high school and attended college at Baylor University in Waco. Nearly four hours away from home, he was free from parental supervision except for our occasional visits and the trips home for which he could prepare and maintain his charade. No one noticed the hideous nettles and poison ivy or pruned the deadly night-shade that was taking over his mind. His self-image was so negative that his own life meant very little to him, and the lives of other people meant even less. He concluded that since we claimed to have given him life, all of his problems were really our fault, and he would be problem-free if we would just disappear.

Maybe he could arrange that.

The first of several attempts on our lives was conceived. The initial ones failed, but the last succeeded. Bart's hard shell cracked when he realized that the plan had actually worked this time, resulting in Tricia's and Kevin's deaths.

It emotionally crippled him for a while in the hospital. Without realizing what was happening, my mother witnessed the first effects of Bart's awakening when he arrived in shock at the emergency room. When she told him that his mom and brother were dead, he began to shake uncontrollably, howling over and over how much he hated "him"—we assumed he meant the shooter, but in reality he was talking about himself. I also saw another early stage of this awakening when Bart retreated into constant sleep in his hospital room, avoiding everyone, including himself. I watched a spiritual darkness closing in on him as he vainly tried to run from the realization of what he had done. Thank God he was not successful.

In a sense the shootings can be viewed as the rain cloud's silver lining, because Bart's spiritual redemption may never have happened without them. This perspective is hard to fathom for anyone without a strong faith in God. Try to look at it this way: You've planned a wonderful trip to Walt Disney World for your family, but your older son is unable to go. This saddens you greatly because you wanted him to experience the magic with the rest of the family, and now he'll miss it. But something comes up, and your wife and younger son leave ten days early—and by doing so, the way opens up for the older son to attend after all. The downside is that for a while, you will miss those who left early. But the joy will be even greater once you and your son join them. The family will be together again.

If you believe in heaven and hell and can view your life through the lens of eternity, what happens on earth is much less important than what happens after you die. Eternity is a long time. In that sense, the shootings and all the horror of the past four years are a small price to pay if they result in Bart's return to the Lord; after all, Tricia and Kevin were going to heaven anyway. They just went early. Although it took the awful experience of betraying his family, abandoning his fiancée, and spending fifteen months in the mountains of Mexico, these were necessary steps in a desperate spiritual journey. Ultimately, I believe December 10 brought back Bart's soul.

All of us who loved Tricia and Kevin have paid a high price in suffering for that purchase, but Bart's soul is more valuable than all of our suffering combined. Bart's redemption and ticket to paradise is God's priceless gift to me. He has given me the deepest desire of my heart by taking the awful events of December 10 and working them together for good, just as he promised. I think that as I lay in the hospital that fateful night, wondering how it could ever be possible to make something good come out of the murders, God was smiling in heaven, saying, "Just you wait and see!"

Nearly a year after fleeing to Mexico, Bart realized he would need to come back to face everyone in order to get their forgiveness and perhaps even be emotionally healed, but as yet he didn't have the internal strength to turn himself in. He chose to wait where he was instead of moving around, knowing that if he stayed, one day the police would come for him. That day came in mid-September 2005.

Chapter 12

THE EVOLUTION OF MURDER

Dan Dunn is a performer who calls his fascinating act Paintjam.

Working with two brushes and a large black canvas that pivots on its center, Dan slings paint onto his medium in time to music, sometimes even using his bare hands to add texture. The early results of his frenetic motion make little or no sense as he turns the canvas this way and that, adding what seem to be random swaths of paint. Then, just as the song is about to end, he adds a line here, rotates the canvas to add a swirl there, and in a flash the subject of the portrait emerges, complete. What had been without meaning for so long suddenly makes sense. You realize that most of the time he had been adding detail upside down or sideways, and your eyes had been tricked.

Like Dan Dunn with his paint, Bart had been filling in detail on a portrait of murder that was hidden from all of us. I think he was painting it even before he realized what it was himself.

THE FIRST ATTEMPT

From Bart's letters, May and June 2007:

> Dad, I am trying to get all this together, but it's hard for me to get my mind back into who I was. I guess we were [in my college] freshman year. I was flaming out of control though I was covering it up well. I surrounded myself (not consciously) with people who were out of control also. People who were depressed and confused, not so I could "manipulate" them as Fred claimed, but because I was less self-conscious around them. Like attracts like. We just found each other. Somewhere in there, I got all twisted up.
>
> I don't know where the idea [for murder] came from. Adam claims we discussed it while working out when I was in eleventh grade, though I don't remember that. Probably it was just another evolution of the game that me and Justin and Will were playing, which was to see who could be the worst. I know for me the plot was never real at first, just a game. Something I could think about when you or Mom bugged me. Again, it was the "If only you knew" game. . . .
>
> I was happy, sort of. As long as the game continued.

Later, when the game started to lose its luster, or broke down completely, I had nothing left. The game of playing evil gave way to the ability to really be evil, by not thinking and just doing.

A well-known psychological law applies equally well to advertising, recreational drugs, saying you're sorry, and any kind of adrenalin rush: the law of diminishing returns says that over time the same stimulus will become less effective in providing the desired results; its corollary is that over time you must increase the dosage of a drug or stimulus to achieve the same effect. For a while just thinking about being free of parental restraints was enough to provide Bart some relief from his self-loathing and disappointment. But as he and his two freshman dorm mates, Will and Justin, shared one another's frustrations, they realized that they were much alike, with similar intellects, resentments, and attitudes. All three were unhappy. Justin had just lost a close friend, who died in a car accident, and didn't seem to care about anything. Will hated being in Waco and was only there because his parents had forced him to go to college. The young men's mutual and unfocused anger slowly worked its way into conversation. During that first year at Baylor, they began to speak more and more about things that should be unthinkable. By the time their sophomore year began, their anger had metastasized into thoughts of murder.

Bart and Justin got an apartment together, and even though Will was no longer in school, he would visit from time to time. The law of diminishing returns had eroded the temporary relief of talking about murder to the point that on one of Will's visits, the boys decided they needed to put the talk into action. They chose December 2000, after classes ended for the semester. Bart would make sure that Kevin was not at home that night.

A plan was set that later evolved into a pattern for multiple murder attempts: Bart would come home and take us to dinner, leaving the back door unlocked and the alarm off. Dressed in black sweats and a ski mask, Will was to be the shooter. He would enter the house, locate the murder weapon (my .22 pistol), and wait for us to come home. Justin would be the lookout and the driver. Bart gave them two of my walkie-talkies so Justin and Will could stay in touch.

What they didn't know was that Bart was changing his mind. He didn't want the attempt to be successful but was afraid of appearing weak in front of the others. Instead of aborting, he just made sure the plan failed.

Bart writes:

> I believe it was a Friday night. Kevin was not to be involved, he was away. Same blueprint as 2003, burglary gone wrong, except the only gun in the picture was your .22, which of course wasn't sufficient. This is one of the points that I remember which bolsters my view that this was more of a bluff than a real attempt—to see how close we could get to the line. Will was supposed to enter from the back door, only I never unlocked it. Nor did I [turn] the alarm off, my only other duty. The game had gone on too far. I didn't turn it off.

But Will was unaware of Bart's change of mind, and persisted. When the back door wouldn't open, he began trying the windows. A small window in our bathroom was unlocked, and when he opened it, the pre-alarm warning was triggered. If Bart's only move to scuttle the attempt had been to leave the doors locked—if he had turned off the alarm as planned—this attempt would have been successful.

Will wiggled halfway through the high window and got stuck, eventually managing to pull himself back outside. He called Justin on the walkie-talkie.

"The alarm wasn't turned off! It's going to start in a minute. What should I do?"

"Oh, man! Okay—forget it and get back to the car before it goes off!"

When we got home from supper, the siren was wailing, but we thought it was just a false alarm. It had happened before, and nothing was missing. Just one of those things that happens sometimes with home alarms.

I had no idea that Mom had left the window unlocked. This wasn't planned, [and Will] couldn't get in the back door. I blamed Will for the screwup to save face with Justin, who thought Will was too weak. Will got mad, went back to Oklahoma, and I never heard from him until the trial. Justin was angry with him, but I think we were both relieved, though we couldn't show this. Randy was correct when he said he thought Justin pushed as hard or harder than I did. Not to take any blame off of me, but this was true.

THE SECOND ATTEMPT

The next attempt would come four months after the first and be much more organized, but it was foiled by a girl who stood on her convictions—and an ignored gas gauge.

Bart writes:

> *I guess most of the discussion was done in the apartment that Justin and I shared. We actually talked about this stuff very seldom. Looking back, both Justin and I were drowning, and we didn't know how to help each other, only make things worse.*
>
> *When [Will] went back to Oklahoma, I went looking for someone else. Adam was the obvious choice, because he was easily the most corrupt person I knew. The second attempt was born when Adam came up to Waco for one of several visits. Justin had the same impression of Adam as I did. He was the ultimate mask-wearer, far more competent at lying than I ever was. Again, I'm not trying to deflect guilt—I accept responsibility for all of this. I just want you to know that none of these other guys were Boy Scouts.*

In January 2001, shortly after the first attempt, Adam met Bart before the two joined other friends from college on a holiday cruise. Justin also met with them, and they discussed plans. Various scenarios were considered, one of which called for Tricia, Kevin, and me to die in a fire at the lake house: Bart would escape with some burns. Adam testified in the trial that this plan was never seriously considered because they couldn't guarantee that all three of us would die. Besides, it would be easy for investigators to recognize arson, and that would quickly lead to suspicion of murder.

Arguments over how to kill us delayed action, but later Adam would visit the others in Waco, where the three finally settled on a plan: Adam agreed to be the killer. Justin would drive from Waco to deliver the murder weapon to Adam, who would then come to our house. The scene would be made to look like a home invasion, with Adam killing us while we slept. If by chance I had already left for work, he would drive across town and kill me there. He would do whatever it took. Bart would be "asleep" in Waco when the call of my death came.

With the basic plan set, the next problem to be faced was obtaining a weapon. The Ruger .22 in my closet wasn't big enough to ensure success. Justin said he could get a gun: "There's a guy in San Antonio who can get whatever we need. That's no problem. Then there won't be any connection to us. Let me see what it's gonna cost."

"Who is this guy?" Adam asked. "Can we trust him?"

"Yeah. I've known him for a while."

"If I'm gonna be Mr. Hit Man, I want to know what your friend's got, get the feel of it. If you guys are serious about this, we need to get moving on it."

As the night wore on, the three worked on other details. Justin would secure the gun from his friend in San Antonio and drive it from Waco to Houston on the night before the scheduled killing. In an effort to further distance themselves from the crime, they decided to steal a car for the trip. Justin had the answer for that too.

"I know a girl who's a dorm RA and has access to lots of cars. She won't care what it's for. She can pull a set of keys from one of the rooms, and we can just unlock it and drive off. I'll be back from Houston before they wake up; she can return the keys, and nobody'll ever know."

By the time Adam left to go home, the plans were complete. The shooting would take place the morning of April 5, 2001.

Sometime around eleven o'clock the night of April 4, as he was getting ready to leave for Houston, Justin had an unexpected visitor. A friend from his high school dropped by after a party and heard him talking with Bart. The boys thought that they had convinced her that she'd misunderstood the conversation and that everything was all right, but after Justin left, this girl had second thoughts and called her boyfriend in Boston.

While the girl and her boyfriend were trying to decide what to do, Justin was on his way to Houston. Next to him on the front seat was a throwaway cell phone and Adam's number. Under it, wrapped in a towel, was the gun. He had only gone a few miles before he encountered a wreck on the freeway that backed up traffic. He finally got around it, but soon the car began to sputter. They had stolen a vehicle with no gas and never checked the gauge. It coasted to a stop on the side of a dark rural road. Justin called Bart.

"Man! You aren't gonna believe this, but that idiot girl got me keys for a car with no gas! I'm dead on the side of the road out in the middle of nowhere! You gotta get here quick!"

"Hang on. I'll be right there."

By this time the girl who'd dropped by the apartment had talked it over with her boyfriend and felt that the police needed to know about the conversation, even if there was nothing to it. They both called the Waco Police Department, who then called the Sugar Land Police Department, who sent a squad car to our house. We didn't believe any of it and tried, unsuccessfully, to reach Bart on his cell phone.

Bart had just finished filling a small gas tank and was nearing Justin's car when Justin did reach him.

"Your dad just called me, man! He wanted to know where you were, and when I told him I didn't know, he handed the phone to a cop. A cop! The Sugar Land police are at your house and want to know if you're in Houston. They asked if I knew anything about murdering your parents! How could they know all this stuff?"

"I can't believe this! Adam must have told somebody. Look, don't answer any more calls. Phone Adam and tell him the deal is busted. I'm turning my phone off. I'll drop off the gas and get back home. You do the same, and get rid of that gun!"

"Right, but I don't think Adam told the cops. I just called him, and he sounded really mad that it wasn't going down. You know him: he was pumped and wanted that money."

Back at the apartment, Bart and Justin spent the rest of the night going over options. They concluded that the leak had to have come from Justin's friend who had overheard them talking. Justin suggested that they tell everyone that the girl had been drinking and had misunderstood an argument between him and Bart about the Menendez brothers, and they agreed to stick with the story.

But Bart felt that he needed more time to think. Things had fallen apart too fast and too completely. It was time to run, just in case the police didn't buy Justin's story. He ended up 140 miles away, north of Dallas, where he stayed for two days. Tricia and I couldn't reach him and were worried sick. When I finally heard from him, he claimed that he had become frightened when he listened to all of the cell phone messages the next morning. He told me that he feared being prejudged because of the break-in at Clements High School two years earlier and that he panicked. I questioned him for a long time and pressed the Waco police for details. After days of investigation, they bought the boys' story about the Menendez brothers and concluded that the event was merely a misunderstanding. I accepted their findings. I knew there were loose ends, but at the time, the police's official explanation seemed more reasonable than the alternative.

We were wrong. The murder attempt was real.

Two attempts had now failed; the next time we wouldn't be so lucky.

EXECUTION

Will had moved home at the end of the semester, in December 2000, following the failure of the first attempt. Justin dropped out of the scene when Bart stopped going to Baylor and transferred to Sam Houston. Adam disappeared into the woodwork after getting Justin's call. They were the lucky ones. They got out without actual blood on their hands and without going to jail. The only punishment they will ever receive on this earth is whatever pain their consciences might bring them at the realization that they once had been ready to kill innocent people for money. That, and the knowledge that Tricia and Kevin might still be alive today if one of them had had the courage to tell someone what he knew.*

Perhaps we could have ended Bart's destructive path with therapy, and we'd still be a family. We could have learned of Bart's fears, and he could have discovered that we would've never abandoned him. Instead, Bart would have two and a half more years to drift further into darkness before the third and final attempt was made. I wonder how the old cast of characters felt when they heard the news.

This time the players had changed, and so had the staging location.

Bart had never been happy at Baylor. Waco was a small town with small-town ways, and Bart liked big-city action and electricity. He saw himself as a cosmopolitan stainless steel rat relegated to a small-town Bible Belt setting. The school was "traditional Baptist," so the ever-present religious undertones were in conflict with Bart's secret rejection of God. But perhaps the main reason for his dissatisfaction was the

---

* The characters who participated in the earlier attempts on our lives are still out there, walking the streets right now. Even though they were involved in actual conspiracies to commit murder, the Fort Bend District Attorney has granted them immunity. None of them has ever tried to contact me or ask for my forgiveness (although Bart, Chris, and Steven have done so).

hypocrisy Bart perceived in many students: outwardly Christian, his friends privately drank heavily, used drugs, and engaged in promiscuous sex. Fair or not, his perception was that the students were hypocrites. It is said that the traits we hate most in others are the traits we hate most about ourselves, and Bart loathed the fact that he was not a real person with a genuine value system. He tried to explain this in one of his letters:

> Baylor was a poison to me. The fakeness of everyone hurt whatever spiritual progress I had made [at the private Christian high school I attended after the public school break-in]. . . . The kids were just like the old [high school] crowd. Maybe a little better behaved in terms of extremes, but worse for the fact that their hypocrisy painted them as something they were not.

By the end of his sophomore year, Bart had found a way to escape Waco: he asked to transfer to Sam Houston State, which is a school about a hundred miles north of Houston and about forty miles from Lake Conroe. He got permission to move into the lake house we shared with Tricia's family and left Waco for good. He would stay at the lake house for a year and a half before moving to a small patio home that Tricia and I bought in anticipation of taking it over as a lake home for ourselves once Bart graduated from college.

Over the course of the next several months, Bart would meet some new friends who became the team that carried out the December 10 murders. The new guys were a little more seasoned, a little more savvy, and a lot more street smart than the kids who'd been involved in the first two attempts. They were just as cynical and morally corrupt, but instead of whining and playing games that got out of hand, as Will and Justin had done, they were much more like Adam, if perhaps not quite as mercenary. The money would be nice, but the experience of killing someone was the real attraction for these two. In fact, specific dollar figures were never discussed.

Chris Brashear was the first to come on board. Bart had been promoted to a food-and-beverage manager in the country club where he worked and was interviewing potential new staff members. He hired Chris as a waiter, a job at which he excelled. They became friends, often meeting socially after work. In time the conversations began to take a familiar turn: living life on the edge, taking chances, and breaking free of society's restrictions. Chris was small in stature but bold and ready for adventure—and eager to prove that he was a dangerous guy. After a few weeks, he moved into Bart's spare bedroom, and they were together most of the time.

One afternoon, as Bart cleaned his patio, a tall, lanky young man approached him. Steven Champagne lived down the street and was dropping by to introduce himself. They hit it off well too, but Steven remained more private and less social than Chris. Like Bart, he kept others at a distance. He came across as someone with a secret, dark past.

A week after Bart hired Chris, he hired Steven as a bartender, and it wasn't long until the three were throwing small parties at Bart's place. As time passed, they grew closer. Dormant for nearly two years, Bart's idea of breaking free from his parents returned. The old plan was resurrected with a team that would finally get the job done.

On the day of the murders, Tricia got a call from Bart saying that he had finished his last exam and wanted to celebrate. She called me, and we agreed on Pappadeaux's restaurant, a family favorite specializing in Cajun-flavored seafood.

With our dinner plans set, Bart picked up Steven and Chris and drove to the Woodlands, a large community just north of Houston and on the way from Conroe. He stole license plates from a parked car in a shopping center, and Steven put them on his mother's Toyota Camry. Bart headed for Sugar Land with Chris hiding on the floor in the back of Bart's Yukon, and Steven following in the Toyota. When he got to our home, Bart went inside and changed clothes while Steven found a place to wait and Chris stayed in Bart's SUV.

By the time I got home from work, it was dark. We gave Bart his graduation present and took some pictures. After we drove off in Kevin's car, Chris got out of Bart's Yukon, hurried to the back door, and entered the house. This time Bart had made sure the back door was unlocked and that the alarm was off. Chris turned off all the lights. Steven waited on the street behind our house for a minute to be sure that Chris got in.

Chris started to put on latex gloves but was shocked to find that he only had one. He must have lost the second one somewhere. Rather than risk being seen, and since he had locked Bart's vehicle when he got out, he went through the house using one hand to open drawers and shuffle stuff around to make it look like a burglary. He then went upstairs and found the gun box in which we kept our Glock 9 mm pistol, right where Bart had told him it would be. He pried it open and loaded the clip with hollow point bullets, specifically designed to expand upon impact and cause maximum internal damage as they passed through the body. Chris had picked them out especially for this job.

In the meantime, Steven followed us to Pappadeaux's, where he located our car and parked in the row behind it, waiting for us to finish eating.

Inside the restaurant, we were enjoying what was to be Tricia's and Kevin's last meal. We shared a lot of laughter and celebrated with a little wine. In retrospect, I recall that Bart's mood shifted from gregarious to quiet and reserved, but it didn't register as anything unusual at the time. I just figured he was tired from his exams. When we finally left the restaurant, we didn't notice the Toyota that pulled out behind us.

Kevin parked in our driveway, and Steven turned down the street behind ours to wait for Chris. We piled out of the car and headed for the front porch, but Bart continued down the driveway to where the Yukon was parked on the street, under the pretense of getting his cell phone that had been charging. I waited for him on the porch as Kevin opened the front door and stepped in, with Tricia right behind him.

When the first shot rang out, I turned from the driveway to the front door. Tricia cried, "Oh, no!" and a second shot followed. Not understanding what was happening, I moved forward and saw inside the house for the first time. Tricia was at my feet, and Kevin lay on the floor twitching as his life ebbed away. But I didn't see them. I saw only a figure in a ski mask, and the next instant I was hit hard in the upper right chest and was knocked on my back. Moments later, a fourth gunshot came from inside the house.

My God, I thought, *he's shot us all.*

I did not see Bart rush into the dark house. I don't know if he looked down at Tricia and Kevin or not, but he ran into the living room, where Chris shot him in the left upper arm . . . according to plan.

Bart's cell phone slipped from his grasp, and Chris dropped the gun, which he was supposed to take with him. Fumbling in the dark for the weapon, he scooped up the phone by mistake and ran out the back door, cracking the top of a fence picket as he raced over it. He dove into the waiting car, and he and Steven sped away. No one noticed them.

Later they told Bart about those first moments after the murders. Both were somber and quiet as the realization of what they had just done settled in. Heading back to Conroe, Steven asked how it went.

"I don't know. I'm pretty sure the mom and Bart's brother are done, but I don't think I finished his dad. I think I got him in the shoulder."

"Well, that's just great. You forgot the gun too, didn't you."

"You think you could have done better? You should have seen his brother. He took it in the chest and fell. He tried to get up once and smiled at me the whole time, with this sad, confused 'I forgive you' smile. God! It gave me the creeps! Then the mom said something, and I shot her. She lay there, but he just flopped around on the ground, bleeding and smiling! I was lucky to hit the dad at all."

"Jesus."

They drove in silence most of the way back to Bart's patio home, where Chris took a shower and changed clothes. For some reason, they then placed all the evidence in plastic Ziploc bags and put those into two canvas duffel bags. They changed the license plates back to their originals and stowed the stolen ones in one of the duffel bags, then drove to a bridge that crossed a three-quarter-mile section of Lake Conroe. Somewhere along that expanse, they threw the duffel bags into the lake, turned around, and drove back to the Ginger Man Bar near downtown Houston, where they got really drunk.

Within a week of the murders, Adam Hipp walked into the Sugar Land Police Department. He had heard about the shootings and recognized the old plan. He asked the detectives if they would be interested in knowing that Bart had talked to him about being the trigger man in a plot two years earlier and gave them some details of the shooting that had not yet been made public. Already they had learned that Bart was not even enrolled in Sam Houston State, let alone ready to graduate as he had told us. Yes, they would be very interested.

They asked if he was there because of the $10,000 reward the City of Sugar Land was offering, since he had not come forward until the reward was announced.

"Well, I don't know about the reward; but I do know my testimony will save the insurance company a lot of money. They should give me $100,000 for saving them so much. That would pretty much pay for the rest of my college. Everybody wins. You solve the case, the insurance company saves nearly a million bucks, and I get a little money for school."

I never learned if they made any deals, but the surprise was on Adam: even if I had died, I only had $50,000 in insurance; Tricia and Kevin had none. He wasn't going to save the insurance company anything. The last I heard, Adam was still trying to collect more than $40,000 from Crime Stoppers. But he told the SLPD what he knew (except for his planned role as the shooter in the second attempt, which he hid from them for a long time) and placed several phone calls to Bart that the police recorded. Although Bart never admitted to anything in those conversations, he did send Adam $250 to stop talking about the shooting and leave him alone. It is safe to say that the investigation moved forward light-years faster thanks to Adam's visit.

Other things fell into place as well. As the police were making their initial crime scene investigation on the night of the murders, one of the officers found Chris's lost rubber glove. It was lying in the street next to Bart's SUV.

They say success comes when opportunity meets preparation. Lead detective Marshall Slot did a masterful job of directing the investigation and later was recognized for his work by being named Sugar Land's Municipal Employee of the Year.

God also rewarded his tenacity by granting him one of the most amazing strokes of "luck" in Texas crime investigation history when police arrested Steven Champagne two years later. Steven agreed to a plea deal and cooperated by telling about the events of December 10. He especially caught Marshall's attention when he mentioned the canvas bags containing all that evidence, protected inside baggies.

Taking their best guess at where along the four-thousand-foot stretch of bridge the bags might have hit the water, detectives dragged the lake unsuccessfully on two occasions. But even in the face of such long odds, Marshall wouldn't give up. The third time was the charm, because at a depth of thirty feet, they found one of the two needles at the bottom of the haystack. Incredibly, the canvas bag was intact and the evidence perfectly preserved in the plastic bags: Chris's prints inside a glove that matched the glove found beside Bart's Yukon. The stolen license plates. The extra ammunition that matched the murder bullets. The disposable cell phones. Clothing that dogs were able to match to Chris's scent from the crime scene. And Bart's cell phone—the one he had lost the night of the shootings and that had been used to call the throwaway phones in the bag.

Bart was now directly tied to the shootings. All that remained was to convict him in court.

But there was one more storm on my horizon.

Chapter 13

48 *HOURS* AND A TRIAL

T wo months before the trial began, Randy McDonald informed me that he had been contacted by a producer for the CBS show *48 Hours Mystery.* Not good news. The last thing I wanted was more exposure; that was one reason we were laboring to avoid a trial. Now it looked like an hourlong program about the murders would be broadcast on national television.

Randy had spent two hours talking to the producer and thought I needed to meet him.

"Randy, I don't want to hear anything from them except that they're staying in New York and not doing the show," I responded. "Can't you discourage them?"

"I knew your feelings, Kent, but they've already made up their minds and are going ahead with it. The judge will allow them to place hidden cameras in the courtroom, and the prosecution has agreed to cooperate. The only question is whether you're going to be a part of it or let Fred Felcman and Marshall Slot be their only interview sources. You might want to think about it."

I stewed for two days, but it all came down to whether the show would be better for our side if I were in it. The family's side of things needed to be presented, but would it be presented fairly? Would CBS use an interview with me to ridicule my act of forgiveness? My support of Bart made no sense to many people, and it would be easy to play that up. Would the producer let me explain God's surprising softening of my heart that allowed me to forgive the shooter on the night of the killings, or would my interview be edited to bash the silly Christian dad who was so consumed with saving his son's life that he was ignoring the son's obvious guilt?

I decided to see what the producer had to say. We met for lunch.

Jay Young was a quiet, pleasant man in his early forties, and I found myself liking him immediately. Polite and relaxed, he didn't fit my mental image of a big-time producer, though Randy told me he had won two Emmys and an Edgar R. Murrow Award for his work on *48 Hours*. I was impressed, but I still worried about the program having a hidden agenda. Sure, Jay was skilled; but was he honest?

"Mr. Young, the truth is that you guys terrify me. How

much would I have to pay CBS to get you to just go away?" I asked, half jokingly.

"I terrify you? Why would you be afraid of me?"

"For one thing, I've seen how the media can cut and paste an interview to achieve whatever points they want to make—and the poor victim can't do anything about it. What if I find out too late that your agenda is to ridicule my faith? I don't wish to offend, but I just don't trust any of the Big Three news departments. I think you guys are much too liberal and have an ingrained secular slant that produces inaccurate news programs."

"I don't know about that, but I honestly have no hidden agenda. Our programs are straight news: we tell the story of a crime and let things fall where they will. The stories don't need embellishment because the truth is fascinating enough. Most of them have an unexpected twist somewhere that sends the program in a surprising direction. Your story, however, is different, in that the facts are pretty straightforward: there's no sudden revelation that sends events spinning. The interesting hook for this program is going to be you."

"Me? Why me?"

"The focus I'll take," he continued, "is the same one you want: your forgiveness. That is what makes this case so different and so interesting. We want to contrast the murders with your response to them. Everybody, at one time or another, has had to either forgive or be forgiven, and you are fascinating proof that it can be done."

If he was telling the truth, this program could be a

powerful national platform to show God's mercy and how he can bring great good from awful things. But what if Jay was just selling me this to get my cooperation? I shot up a quick prayer for guidance and decided to test his sincerity.

"Jay, if I agree to an interview, will you promise me in writing that the final, as-aired program will include two things: the Christian story of sin, forgiveness, and the need for salvation; and my story of how God supernaturally gave me the ability to forgive the unforgivable, when at the time all I wanted was revenge? Without them, my actions make no sense, and it would be impossible to give an honest portrayal of my story."

"Sure, I'll agree to that because it's what I want too. I want the viewers to hear your story. I'm not sure how your faith has been able to get you through this, but I am fascinated, and if I do my job right, I think the viewers will be too. I have no hidden agenda and will even put that in the letter, if you like."

Over the next four or five weeks, Jay and I met three more times to prepare for the interviews. He wanted to tape me just before the trial began, and again just after it ended. I guess they wanted to see if my attitude would change.

While Jay and I were getting to know each other better, Randy was busy with jury selection, which began on January 22, 2006. Bart was present, and since the judge allowed him to wear street clothes, once a week I brought him a fresh change. He and I went over clothing options and settled on two conservative suits and a variety of dress shirts. I realized that regardless of how the trial went, this was probably the last time in his life that Bart would ever wear something other than prison garb. Knowing how much he used to like nice clothes, I was surprised at how little importance he seemed to place on them now. Whichever shirts I chose were fine with him.

Randy had warned me that as a witness I wouldn't be able to observe any of the trial until I was released from my obligation to testify. I was in a unique position, since I wore three distinct and conflicting hats: I was the chief victim, the primary prosecution witness, and the main witness for the defense. Randy said he had never seen a trial in which one person was in such a triple-edged situation. Until I could no longer be called as a witness, both sides were going to be vigilant to protect my testimony from becoming tainted. This meant that once the trial started, I wouldn't be allowed to hear any details of what was happening, including newspaper or television reports.

It also meant that I wouldn't be able to attend the jury selection. While I wouldn't have wanted to sit through all of it, I would have enjoyed watching Randy and Bart work together in this phase. Just before the trial began, Randy told me that he had never worked with anyone—lawyer, jury selection expert, or anyone—who was better at helping him choose jurors. He came to value Bart's input as they discussed pros and cons for each candidate. Just another of a hundred little things to remind me what a waste Bart had made of his life.

Randy called from time to time to let me know how the jury selection process was going. Before it began, he had told Fred that he was going to be very deliberate and that it might take as long as ten weeks to seat a jury. But as the candidates came and went, things proceeded much quicker than expected, and the jury was empaneled in about a month. It looked like we were going to have a trial.

Randy was pleased with the group that had been selected, pointing out that it was filled with strong personalities who would not be easily swayed. This was important: even though this trait could work against us, he wanted people who, if they came to agree with us that pursuing the death penalty in this case was unfair, would hold out for life in prison. He felt that we had about as good a chance with these people as we could hope for.

As the trial and my first interview with *48 Hours* loomed closer, I considered how best to prepare. My personality is what I call the "mastery" type, which likes to prepare for conflict with study and practice. This is in contrast to the "challenge" type, who doesn't like to be bothered with details but wants to just jump in and make the sale. I have never felt confident as an extemporaneous speaker, and testifying in my son's murder trial against a professional debater was about as extreme an extemporaneous situation as I could imagine. How could I possibly prepare for that?

I realized that I couldn't. In prayer, I asked for God's help—and I got an answer, but not one I was expecting.

I believe God was telling me to trust him and not to practice at all. I was to go into both the interview and the trial relying totally on his provision.

I remembered another man who had faced an authority with power to decide the fate of an entire nation. At least I didn't stutter, as he had! In that situation, Moses tried to back

out of his upcoming showdown with Pharaoh, telling God
he was the wrong man for the job. But God told him not to
worry about what to say, because he would put the words into
Moses' mouth. This gave me a lot of encouragement. I asked
God to do for me what he had done for Moses. I looked at my
interview with *48 Hours* and my testimony in court as a way
to share whatever message God wanted me to share, just as
Moses' confrontation had accomplished God's will long ago.
Since I had no specific idea of what God wanted to accomplish, I had no clue what he wanted me to say—which would
have made rehearsal difficult anyway. So I simply prayed that
God would grant me peace and give me the strength of my
convictions, trusting him to come through.

When I stepped onto the witness stand on Monday, February 26, I probably set a record for lack of preparation by a
key witness in a murder trial. Not only had I chosen to rely on
God's help rather than to rehearse possible examination strategies, but I also had received no preparatory coaching from
Randy. From the beginning, he had told me that my strength
as a defense witness was my character and my faith. He just
wanted me to be myself and tell the truth, not worrying about
where the prosecution was heading with their questions or
trying to evaluate what would be the best answer. He knew
I would face hard questions that required embarrassing answers about Bart's past, but he also felt it was important for
the jury to understand that I was transparent in my testimony
and in my life. They needed to see that my forgiveness was
exactly what it appeared to be and that it was given in spite
of how hard the deaths had been on me—and even though

I acknowledged all that Bart had done. So when I sat in that witness seat, the extent of my preparation was a lot of prayer that God would put the right words on my lips.

I felt the tension of anticipation, just as I used to feel before an important confrontation at work or one of the big bicycle tours. But it wasn't fear. I felt calm and a sense of confidence because I had already experienced God's guidance in my initial *48 Hours* interview three days earlier.

On the Friday morning before the trial, my home temporarily became a television studio. By nine o'clock three of my friends, two cameramen, two soundmen, a producer, an interviewer, and $350,000 worth of video equipment were in my living room. It took two and a half hours to get the lighting just right, but by noon we were ready to go.

I was interviewed by Peter Van Sant, a regular on the program. He has been doing interviews for years and is good at putting people at ease. We got to know each other while the crew was setting up, and I can honestly say that I think he would make a great neighbor. He treated me with respect and compassion, but in six hours of taping, he also deftly probed sensitive and emotional areas. There wasn't much that he missed, and at times the questions made me uncomfortable, but I never felt he took advantage of me.

During that long day I was amazed by the sense of God's presence. While every comment came from my heart, I could feel him helping me choose the right words, and they flowed smoothly. I smiled to myself when I realized this was how

Moses must have felt as he argued with Pharaoh. In what could have been a terribly stressful experience, I was energized and relaxed. When it was over I knew that God had been faithful . . . and that he would show up for the trial too.

I was the first witness to be sworn in, and the prosecution began its examination. Again I felt God directing my thoughts and words, and often I was surprised at my own responses to Fred's questions. For example, we had an exchange concerning the money Bart used to finance his escape to Mexico.

Before Bart ran away, I had argued that he should stay and fight any charges—I didn't want him bolting like he had done when he fell under suspicion in Waco. Yet I also had reminded him of a significant amount of cash that I had set aside several years earlier in anticipation of possible Y2K problems. I can't reconcile or justify these conflicting actions. On one hand I'd warned Bart against running, but on the other I'd pointed out that cash was readily available.

At the time, I felt torn because I didn't know if he was innocent or guilty. I could see every side of the question but couldn't see which argument was the right one. If he was innocent, I wanted him to fight to clear his name. But I also knew that innocent people sometimes get convicted on circumstantial evidence. If he was innocent and could make a new life somewhere else in the world, it might be better than risking conviction in our imperfect legal system. If Bart was guilty, he owed it to everyone to take his medicine, yet I didn't want to see my only remaining son put to death. To my shame and in my weakness, I found myself reminding him of the money.

Fred pursued this, asking why I had not told the police about the missing money; and I finally admitted that if Bart was innocent, I didn't want him to have to fight this. Then Fred asked, "And that's why you didn't tell the police that he took the money?"

Without thinking, the words just came out: "No, it was because of a moral failure on my part."

I think I was as surprised as he was. While this was exactly what I was feeling, I don't think I had ever looked at it that way. Fred stared blankly at me for what seemed like several seconds, and then went on to a different line of questioning.

I never got angry or frustrated, which I easily might have done, considering the personal and combative nature of the questions. My answers came smoothly and effectively. For example, I was able to segue from one of Fred's comments to how strongly both families opposed the pursuit of the death penalty. I stressed how unnecessary we felt the trial was, since the prosecution had known for a year and a half that Bart wanted to plead guilty if they would just drop the death penalty.

I also was able to counter Fred's misrepresentation of why I opposed the death penalty. "Mr. Felcman," I said, "you have implied that I am a good man who loves his son so much that I have a blind eye to the horror of what happened and his involvement. That is completely untrue. Every aspect of my life was changed on December 10, and I am intimately aware of it.

We never claimed Bart's innocence in planning these murders; he remained silent when arraigned because he didn't want to lie. The judge had to enter a plea of not guilty for him. His guilt has never been in question, only the punishment that is being pursued.

"The reasons I have vigorously fought against the death penalty in this case are multiple. Of course I love my son and don't want to see him die, but that is perhaps only twenty percent of the reason. My main objections stem from my Christian faith, which tells us that when we die, we will all begin a second life in one of two places: either with God in heaven or separated from him forever in hell. Our faith also tells us that everyone has sinned—you, me, Bart, all of us— and that God cannot coexist with sin. If any of us are going to heaven, we must first have that sin removed from our soul. The foundational tenet of the Christian faith is that sin must be paid for, and people can't do it themselves. Only by faith in Jesus can those sins be removed, because only Jesus has lived a sinless life. The bonus is that once we ask Christ to be our Lord and Savior and are forgiven for our sins, we also become a new creation with a new heart: we are not the same people we used to be.

"I can't read my son's heart. While I believe he is now saved and has been changed into a new man, only he and God know the truth. What if he isn't and it takes him as long as it took me to reach that decision? I was nearly forty years old before I knew for certain that I was saved, and if you have your way, he'll be executed long before he gets that old. I want him to have as much time as possible to make that decision, if it has not already been made. If it has been made, and he has been saved, I want him to have as much time as possible to do good works and reach others for Christ, even though it will all have to be done from within prison. I'm not so much interested in what happens in this life, except for how it affects the next one. I'm trying to give him as much time as possible to prepare for eternity."

My testimony lasted from ten thirty until about two o'clock that afternoon, but eventually it was over. Walking out of the courtroom into the glare of camera lights, I felt that I had done what God wanted me to do. I just wished I knew what his plans were.

I wouldn't be called back to testify until the following Wednesday, and during that time I didn't watch any news or read any of the papers. A friend or two would call each day with general updates, but that was all. Once the trial was over, I learned that at least five friends and family members had attended every minute, and as Matt Barnhill later told me, it was the hardest thing he had ever endured. The horror of it all affected everyone. I guess it was a blessing that I missed it.

Once the prosecution finished with me, they brought in a series of people, from Steven Champagne (who was charged as the driver) to police officers, previous conspirators, and Bart's former friends and coworkers. As we had known for months, their case was tight and complete. The only real question was whether we could get at least one of the jurors to hold out for a sentence of life in prison. It looked like it was going to be close.

Chapter 14

THE VERDICT

I remember the first time I saw the courtroom, long before the trial began. I couldn't believe it was so small.

It held only five pewlike benches, and two were reserved for members of the press and court officials. If everyone in Fort Bend County who had expressed an interest actually showed up, it was going to get really crowded. When I learned that only thirty seats would be available for the public, I was appalled. Fortunately, the district attorney's office provided a victim's rights advocate to assist victims' families in trials like this. I think it was a little out of the ordinary for the victims' families to be pulling for the defense, but Wanda Greenbaugh, our advocate, was delightful and didn't seem to mind. She proved to be an invaluable help. For starters, she petitioned the judge and was able to reserve ten seats each day for both my family and Tricia's. All I had to do was coordinate who would be there each day, since the bailiff needed specific names in order to issue seating passes.

The next week and a half was rough sledding for everybody. On most days I was able to fill all ten of my family's seats, and several other friends sat with Tricia's family. But the never-ending parade of awful testimony was hard on everyone who attended. My friends told me that it was torture having to hear the terrible details of how our beloved Tricia and Kevin had died and about how the Bart they all loved had made two other attempts to arrange for the murder of his family. Some who had told me they were planning to attend more than once found that they just couldn't do it. By Friday, when both sides rested in the guilt-or-innocence phase, we all were exhausted. I was only able to fill eight of the ten seats, and because no one had claimed them, those two empty seats became the focus of a Friday-afternoon blowup.

Closing arguments were set to begin Monday morning, and a speedy verdict was expected. Since I was still waiting to be called as a witness for the defense, I would not be allowed into the courtroom to hear the closing arguments. But even though I would not be physically present, I was nonetheless drawn into a bit of drama.

On Friday afternoon, as both sides ended testimony and prepared to leave for the weekend, one of my friends called with some shocking news.

"Kent, as we were leaving they told us that all of the seats for Monday were already taken. The police department got them all."

"What?! How can they do that? Those twenty seats have been reserved for us—they can't just take them. Besides, even the ten unassigned seats are supposed to be on a first-come first-serve basis—they can't get them in advance like that!"

I was furious. I could see what the police were trying to do. If they were successful in securing all of Monday's seats, they could fill them with uniformed officers, showing solidarity with the prosecution. A sea of black uniforms would be the last thing the jury saw as they filed out. And not only would they be visible, but we would not be. On one of the most important days of the trial, my friends and family would not be allowed inside the courtroom. Suddenly I was back in battle mode. This would not stand. I asked to speak with Wanda, our advocate with the DA's office.

"Wanda, you may not know it yet, but those seats you arranged for our families have been given to the police. Can you find out what happened? This is absolutely wrong and against the seating rules we were given—whether innocent or not, it smacks of special privilege. How can they do this? Every morning for the last five days, I have had to submit a list of the people using our seats because the bailiff wouldn't let me assign them in advance. And now all our seats have been assigned away from us three days early? How did this happen?"

Even through my anger, I felt sorry for Wanda. I think this development had surprised her as much as it did me. She said she would talk to the judge's assistant and the bailiff to see what she could do. When she came back to the phone, she didn't know much more except that the police had requested and received the seats for Monday because we had not filled all ten of our allotted seats on Friday.

"Wanda, I understand that they want to fill the court, and I have no objection to their getting all of the open seating if ten officers show up Monday morning and are first in line, just like everyone else. But I strongly object to their being able to reserve seats in advance when no one else has been able to do so all week. And I am furious that they have somehow been able to circumvent the rules and steal the seats that the judge reserved for us. Now I learn that my family and friends are going to be barred from attendance on the day my son's guilt or innocence will be decided, apparently because the Sugar Land Police Department pulled strings with the court for a show of force? What sort of message does this send?"

Wanda promised to see what she could do and again put me on hold for several minutes. After a great deal of back-and-forth, a compromise was reached. The police would not get every seat, after all. On Monday the ten unassigned seats that would normally be given on a first-come first-serve basis would be held for our families instead, and the police would also give back a few of our seats. Our families' available seating numbers were reduced, and we would have to sit in the back row instead of closer to the front, but at least the room would not be an uninterrupted sea of black uniforms. Just half a sea.

In retrospect, I am ashamed at how I reacted. Yes, it was the department's petty attempt to fill the room, but it definitely wasn't the Watergate I felt it to be that afternoon. I have asked myself why I reacted so explosively, and I believe it was transference of anger that really should have been directed at Bart. Since Christmas I had bottled that up because the trial was approaching and I didn't want to give the prosecution any additional ammunition; I already felt as outgunned as Colonel Travis at the Alamo, and I didn't want the prosecution misunderstanding my anger at him as a wavering of my support. I was angry at the DA for forcing the case into trial, but I really should have been angry at Bart for committing the awful crime that made that possible. Subconsciously, I would not let myself direct the anger at Bart as I should have, and it spilled out against the police. At the time, they were a safe target; I am sorry for the cheap shots I took.

As expected, on Monday the jury did not need to deliberate long after hearing the closing arguments before they returned a guilty verdict. Whether he was guilty was never really the question, since he had not pleaded innocent and Randy had not fought against the prosecution's basic presentation of their very strong case. Our whole focus would be on the penalty phase. But even though the ruling was a mere formality, it brought home once again that this surreal trip was indeed reality.

Arguments to decide whether Bart lived or died would begin the following morning, when Randy began presenting witnesses for the defense.

From the beginning Randy planned to avoid using expert witnesses to explain Bart's behavior. While we believed that compelling arguments could be made to explain Bart's actions, Randy knew that the prosecution would also bring experts in who would draw far different conclusions. I was in favor of having Bart tested by a psychiatrist, but Randy believed this would be legal suicide. Psychology is more art than science, and the same test results can lead different examiners to make vastly different diagnoses. The evidentiary case against Bart was solid and the crime was horrible; at all costs we needed to keep the prosecution from being able to claim through an expert witness that Bart was a psychopath or something similar. Even if our expert could argue otherwise and show that Bart's personality of three years earlier had been permanently altered by subsequent events, the jury would still be faced with having to choose between testimonies from opposing experts. So Randy suggested that we focus on the few positives we had: Bart's family and his change in demeanor.

Randy called Tricia's brother to be the first defense witness in the punishment phase, and he pleaded eloquently for a life sentence. We still had hope that at least one of the jurors would hold out against the death penalty; if that happened, Bart would automatically receive life in prison with little chance of ever getting out. Focusing on how difficult an execution would be on the family, my brother-in-law said that we had suffered enough. A life sentence would allow the family to achieve closure now and would still protect society, since Bart would probably never be released. If Bart were given the death penalty, none of us would be able to have that closure for perhaps another six years; and the whole ordeal would be kept constantly in front of us as the appeals process ground slowly along.

After completing his testimony, Tricia's brother was released, and I was called back to the stand.

This time I testified for only about an hour. I was again filled with peace, knowing that God was right there with me. Again I sensed him leading me in responding, and I felt confident and relaxed even under the painful questioning. I identified with Daniel in the Old Testament when he spent the night in the den of hungry lions: we both would have rather been somewhere else, and we both were aware of what a dangerous place it was, but we also felt a great peace and assurance knowing that God was by our side.

When I stepped down from the witness stand, I was able to take a place in the spectator benches for the first time. As I walked toward them, I hoped I would never have to testify again.

I had barely reached my seat when Randy called Bart to testify. I had known that he might do this, although he never told me for certain. It was a big gamble to put Bart on the stand because it would allow the prosecution to attack him directly for the first time in the trial. But Randy thought it was worth the risk. He wanted the jury to see that Bart was truly repentant and that he should not be considered a continuing threat. He wanted them to see that Bart was taking full responsibility for everything that happened. Electric tension filled the room as Bart was sworn in.

Bart was polite and respectful under Randy's questioning; he answered clearly and honestly, never once making excuses. I thought surely the jury would see that these responses could not have come from the damaged young man who had been so lost three years ago. Surely they would realize that God had been at work in his heart and that he had changed. Randy asked Bart about many things, trying to show that the dark place in which Bart had been three years earlier had come from human failings and misunderstandings about the relationships within his family. Those misunderstandings would never apply to others; his family had been the target of his misplaced hate, and he had no reason to extend such hatred to others. Besides, Randy and Bart contended, the mind that had constructed these misunderstandings was no longer capable of doing so again. I hoped this exchange would be enough to show that Bart would not present a danger to the public.

Mr. Felcman's cross-examination was exactly what one would expect: well done, and difficult for me to endure. Time after time Bart would try to answer the broad and accusatory questions, only to have his comments interpreted in the most negative light. At every opportunity Bart admitted his guilt and claimed to be the one most responsible for the murders, never making excuses, but it didn't seem to matter. At one point Fred startled everyone by slamming his hand down on the jury box, emphasizing his anger and outrage at Bart's actions. Everyone in the room jumped. Fred did everything to break Bart's concentration and to draw conclusions that changed what Bart had said. Each time, Bart did his best to politely explain to Fred. I was amazed at how he was able to hold back his anger; I was having a hard time with mine!

It seemed to me that Mr. Felcman was putting a negative spin on everything Bart said. Of course, as a prosecutor, that is his job. But I think there was more going on than just being a good prosecutor. I think they were both being honest—it was as if there were two different languages being used. Fred never believed that Bart could possibly have been changed by his encounter with God in Mexico, and Bart could never convince him that he was no longer the awful person who had planned the murders. At one point Fred expressed his moral outrage by saying that dealing with people like Bart tainted his soul and that he looked ten years older because of it.

He finished by arguing that Bart was incapable of change: he never had changed and never would. He pointed out that my family and Tricia's were nice people who didn't deserve what we had gone through but that our concerns were not what the jury was called to address. They were to decide whether Bart was a continuing threat to society, and Fred charged that Bart's actions leading up to the shootings had shown that he was. The only way to protect the general population within the Texas prison system was to execute him.

Randy called no other witnesses, so on that note the defense rested. Closing arguments would be the following morning, and then the jury would deliberate over Bart's fate.

The next morning I met several friends at a Mexican café for breakfast, but we were all so nervous that no one could eat. So we drank strong coffee and watched one another get wound up even tighter. Eventually nine o'clock rolled around, and we filed through the cameras and reporters into the courtroom.

I didn't really know what to expect, having never sat through an actual trial before. The experience was instructive.

Jeff Strange, who had helped Fred in the prosecution, began by presenting thirty minutes of well-organized summation that can be distilled into three points: Bart was irreparably sick; he was only interested in himself; and he had repeatedly tried to arrange these murders until they finally happened, because he wanted the money. It was all about the money. My son was cold-blooded and would be until he died.

I had great hopes when Randy began his summation, but I was quickly disappointed. For one thing, I could barely hear him. The courtroom was designed with hidden microphones that picked up what was spoken so the gallery could hear, but they were directional and thus only effective in a few places. If you stood (as Randy was doing) in an area that was "dead," only the judge, jury, and those in front of the public seating area could hear well.

Randy had told me that his focus that day would be on the members of the jury who might hold out for life in prison, and he thought three or four of them might. While he directed his summation at them, the frustration of those of us watching increased because we kept waiting for him to do the impossible: make a grand Perry Mason move. By the time Randy completed his hour of summation, I felt deflated.

Fred then spent the last thirty minutes of the prosecution's court time focusing on how evil and cunning Bart was, how he had always been that way and always would be. He became more and more animated, arms waving and voice rising as he spoke of how cold and manipulative Bart was. In the end, just before his time ran out, Fred finished by breaking down in tears.

I was shocked at what I had just witnessed.

The jury received its charge and filed out.

I was a little numb. Of course, everything that the prosecution had said was true as it applied to Bart three years
earlier. No arguments from me. I lived every day with the consequences of his actions. I knew how evil the murders were.
But I felt empty as I realized that (at least in that small part
of the trial I had witnessed) the defense had been ineffective
in showing how Bart had changed, in spite of the many de-
monstrable things that proved that change. For the first time,
I had a sick feeling that things were not going to end as I had
hoped and expected. Even if some jurors wanted to hold out
against the death penalty, I feared that they had not been
given enough evidential ammunition to withstand a vigorous
opposition in the deliberation room.

After working our way back outside through the camera
lights, soundmen, and reporters, all of whom wanted my
thoughts, seven or eight of my friends met me at the Italian
Maid Cafe for lunch. My first remarks addressed the growing
fear that Bart would receive the death penalty.

"Guys, I had hoped that the closing arguments would
give me more hope. But it's over, and at some point the jury is
going to come back with a verdict. I need help here: What do I
say, either way?"

Matt Barnhill replied, "Just tell them what you've been
saying all along."

"Matt! I'm the guy who can't even decide what I'm going
to have for lunch, remember? I need some help here! What
have I been saying all along?"

"That you have prayed from the very beginning that God
would do whatever he needed to do to reach Bart. You believe

that God is in charge, and so you believe that this verdict is God's will."

As usual, Matt saw through to the crux of the problem and came up with a solution. The truth is, I had been saying that since day one. And I still believed it—whichever way the jury went.

We ordered lunch, and after a while Randy dropped by, confessing that he didn't feel he'd done his best work that morning. I shared that we had just been talking about how we all believed that God was in charge, so not to worry, regardless of what happened. I said I trusted him and wouldn't have traded him for any other attorney. Well, maybe Johnnie Cochran. We all laughed.

Randy left and, with lunch over, the rest of us sat around and visited, waiting for word that the jury had made a decision. Time passed, and suddenly we realized we'd been sitting at the table for six hours. We left the restaurant and strolled down the small-town street for a few blocks, admiring the hundred-year-old storefronts and ancient trees. The sky grew dark and the air cool, so around eight o'clock we ventured into another restaurant for supper. There we came across more friends and some of Tricia's family. Still no word from the jury.

An hour later, just as we were about to go home, we learned that the jury had asked for some specific testimony and that we should wait a while longer, in case the verdict was reached that night. Wanda showed us to some offices where we could wait out of the chilly night air and away from the news cameras. By now a few of the friends from lunch had gone home, and a few others had joined us. Even if bad news came tonight, I would not be alone. But at 10:45 p.m. Wanda told us that the jury was quitting for the night and would be back in the morning. It was a positive sign. The group broke up, and I drove wearily home. It had been a long day.

The next morning was beautiful. I told myself that if we could make it through one more day without a verdict, Bart might have a chance.

Four friends met me in the parking lot, and we entered the courthouse together, prepared for another extended period of waiting. Wanda met us in the hall and offered to let us stay in an office they normally used for interviews with abused kids. We sat in chairs facing one another and engaged in small talk until Matt noticed a few games on a bookshelf otherwise filled with children's books. I half-jokingly suggested that we all play Candy Land, and to my surprise my friends Charlene, Arnold, and Doris agreed. Matt spent his time reading in the corner as the rest of us pretended we were preschoolers. Except I don't think preschoolers ever took the game so seriously.

The mind is a strange thing. I needed to be distracted so I wouldn't think of the time slowly ticking away—and about what might be coming. Under the right circumstances, even a game designed for five-year-olds can do the trick. We had great fun! Laughing, creating alliances, and keeping track of who had done what to whom, we were starting the fourth game when Wanda stuck her head into the room. Suddenly everything was serious again.

"We have a verdict."

I looked at the clock: it was only eleven. That was a bad sign. It was too soon for the jury to have given up after a deadlock, so this meant they had reached a decision . . . and it didn't take a genius to figure out that the odds favored death.

As I entered the courtroom, I saw the faces of many of my friends and loved ones. They had been wonderfully faithful, and now the ordeal was going to end, one way or another.

While we waited for the jury, Randy came over and whispered to me that the verdict would be the death penalty. He said that at one point yesterday, the jury had been evenly divided 6–6. But as the evening wore down, so did the resolve of those holding out for a life sentence. The jury foreman, in particular, was forceful in pressing for the death penalty. (Later I would learn that his statement to the media was, "Bart cannot change. It is impossible for him to change. I hope he finds God!" How ironic that this is what had already happened, and yet the foreman didn't know it.) One by one the holdouts changed their minds, until only two remained firm at the end of the evening. Within hours of returning to deliberations the next morning, the last two were finally swayed. What I had feared in my worst nightmares was coming true.

Thirty minutes that felt like an eternity passed before the bailiff called us to rise for the judge and jury. Later Charlene pointed out that I had nervously bounced my leg up and down the whole time, but I didn't notice it. One by one the three charges were answered by the jury foreman: no, there were no extenuating circumstances; yes, Bart would be a continuing threat to others; and yes, although he had not actually pulled the trigger, Bart knew that his involvement would lead to murder.

It was official now. The judge told Bart to rise and formally sentenced him to be remanded into the custody of the Texas prison system until an execution date could be set, at which time he would be injected with lethal chemicals until he was pronounced dead. Bart was taken away. I had not touched my son since he ran off to Mexico nearly three years before. And now I never would.

It was over.

Wanda kindly asked if I wanted to wait until everyone else had left before I went outside. Out of courtesy to me, everyone waited for my decision, but I decided that I might as well go first. That way perhaps the cameras would leave everyone else alone. Flanked by my friends, I stepped out into the hallway, which was jammed with media. Big Arnold, looking like Michael Clarke Duncan, the brawny actor from *The Green Mile* and *Armageddon*, strode through them, opening a path to the elevator for the rest of us. As he pushed the button, I gave my statement.

"This is a sad day. It is a sad day for everyone. From the very beginning I have prayed that God would do whatever it took to reach my son. While this was not the verdict that we had hoped for, I still believe that the Lord is sovereign, and I believe that his will was done today. There will be no further statement by me, my family, or Tricia's. I respectfully ask that you grant us the courtesy of respecting our privacy."

The elevator door opened after what seemed like hours,

and in moments we were finally out of the building. I never want to set foot in it again.

Our plan was for Charlene to pick up some lunch for all of us, and we would meet at Matt's house to debrief. Once Matt and I were safely in his car, I felt a strange combination of crushing sadness and guilty relief wash over me. It was finished: there was nothing else for me to do. I was no longer Bart's champion, because all options had been tried. All that remained was for me to be his father and friend.

An image took shape in my mind of Bart on a gurney, looking at me through the glass as his eyes glazed over.

I would be his friend for as long as I could.

Chapter 15

SIX YEARS TO ETERNITY

The little boy lost in the lonely fen,
Led by the wand'ring light,
Began to cry, but God ever nigh
Appeard like his father in white.

He kissed the child & by the hand led
And to his mother brought,
Who in sorrow pale, thro' the lonely dale,
Her little boy weeping sought.

—William Blake, "The Little Boy Found"

What do you do when the life of someone you love becomes a train wreck?

For years my route to work paralleled a heavily used train corridor. One morning, about fifteen years ago, I came upon a bizarre scene just as the sun was coming up: sometime during the night, a large freight train had jumped the tracks. About twenty tankers and gravel cars were piled atop one another as if they had been carelessly tossed into a child's toy box. Twisted rails and splintered cross ties were strewn everywhere, as were detached wheels and spring assemblies. Great mounds of dirt had been gouged from the earth, some train cars partly buried beneath them while others lay sideways under their neighbor's cargo. Miraculously, the highway had escaped damage, but the devastation came within a few feet of the road and stretched for hundreds of yards along the track. I was reminded of the train-wreck scene from *The Fugitive* as I tried to imagine what it must have been like to witness this mass collision.

Months would pass before the wreckage was all cleared and the track relaid. It took even longer for the deep scars in the earth to be smoothed away.

The trial was like that. All of the trauma of December 10, 2003, and the terrible months and years after it came crashing back, played out before the five million people served by Houston television. The wreckage was everywhere: television, radio, newspapers, and casual conversations. Once the verdict was handed down, there was nothing left to do but go on living and try to clean up. The emotional scars from the murders, their consequences in our families' lives, and the horrible experiences of the grand jury and the trial will never completely disappear. Our new "normal" lives are a lot different from our old ones.

Bart was sent to the Polunsky Unit of the Texas Department of Corrections, which is located near Livingston, about two hours from my home. Thank goodness the unit is reasonably accessible and not a twelve-hour drive away, like Lubbock or El Paso. About 370 men are on Texas's death row now, including my son, and they are all housed in Polunsky. No place else is quite like it.

Unlike in any other prison setting in Texas, no physical contact between inmates is allowed: each man is kept locked in his individual ten-by-six-foot cell, twenty-four hours a day. They read, write letters, sleep, and think. They have no assemblies, no movie nights, no television, no communal dining, and no jobs. No one receives training in anything, since these men have no future. Even church services are forbidden now because that would allow inmates to gather together. These men are simply being warehoused in isolation until their appeals expire and the state is finally allowed to execute them.

Three days a week inmates are taken out of their cells for two hours and placed, alone, in an exercise room. A second inmate is in a bordering exercise room separated by a metal fence and a concrete wall; this is the closest death-row prisoners ever get to social contact. The men usually spend most of their exercise time talking to each other through the fence because human contact is so precious and limited. Besides, they have little else to do during that time: the rooms had been emptied of exercise equipment about the same time church services were discontinued.

Perhaps the authorities decided that the weights and other equipment could be thrown at the concrete walls and damage them, or perhaps they just wanted to punish the convicts in yet another way. Such attitudes are common. Whatever the reason, this limits exercise to push-ups, sit-ups, and jogging in place, all of which can be done in their cells.

Twice a week prisoners get solitary exercise time in a special area open to the sky. This is the only time in their weekly routine that these men get exposure to outside air; even so, since this area is essentially the bottom of a thirty-foot well, direct sunlight is experienced only when the inmate's time there coincides with the sun being directly overhead. If the weather is cold or rainy, or if the temperature reaches one hundred degrees (which happens frequently in the summer), an inmate can choose to skip his "outside" time and remain in his cell.

Don't get me wrong: I know prison was never intended to be a Holiday Inn. But these harsh and emotionally numbing conditions would never have been allowed back when the U.S. Department of Justice had oversight over the Texas prison system.

This will be Bart's life as the automatic appeals process winds through the court system. The two appeals, and the time the state allows for them, were streamlined during George W. Bush's tenure as governor. Average time is now six years.

But in some ways, being on the Row has advantages. For one, it's the safest place in the Texas prison system. While gang membership still affects prisoners' lives (even in these segregated conditions), it does not bring the chaos that exists elsewhere. It's much harder to initiate hostilities or retaliate with such limited contact. The guards generally travel in pairs, which helps to curb corruption. Another benefit is that this is the only place in the entire Texas prison system where inmates live in air-conditioning. In all other units, the cells have barred windows that are open to the elements to allow air circulation; but since there are no opening windows in the Row, the state makes an attempt to regulate air temperature with minimal AC.

Bart seems to have settled in. He has changed dramatically. Gone are the arrogance and posturing of old, as well as the masks; he is open, repentant, and accepting of where he is. He recognizes how lucky he is to have had his relationship with God restored. One of his greatest disappointments is that he has so little opportunity to witness to other inmates and share how his experience has changed his life. He wrote of this frustration in one of his letters:

> *I came here with my heart set on doing God's work, totally devoted. I felt this is where he wanted me. And yet there are so few opportunities to do anything here. There's so little time to socialize and share the Word. . . . And honestly, most of these men already believe in God. Those who don't have very specific and detailed reasons for not believing. What do I say in two hours to guys who have never had a day of happiness in their whole lives, until one day they blew up?*

I didn't have the answer when he wrote that, and I still don't. But we both believe that he is there for a reason and that it eventually will be revealed. I am convinced that God will work Bart's conviction and move to death row for good. I think it is instructive to note that the last person Jesus forgave before he died was a repentant criminal hanging next to him.

That man freely confessed his sin—and the appropriateness of his execution—just as Bart has done. While the forgiven sinner on the cross traded this earthly life for paradise that same day, Bart has been left to live for a time. We believe that God will use this time to accomplish his purposes just as he has used me to reach Bart and to encourage others.

As I look back at the last four years, I am amazed at how God has worked. In a strange way, my story should encourage everyone who is facing hardships that make no sense, whether they are medical, relational, or financial. All of us have at times worried about potential catastrophes and wondered if we would be able to rebuild should disaster strike. My story might be the ultimate parental nightmare. What could be more heartbreaking than to have your son kill his mom and little brother, and try to kill you . . . and then suddenly abandon you, taking your money and leaving you with all the loose ends . . . only to be arrested and then try to confess but be forced through a media trial (and its associated huge financial drain) that was unnecessary?

I have had hundreds of people tell me that my story makes their troubles pale in comparison. But what lesson can we learn from my experiences?

Perhaps it is that we always have the power of choice: to trust or not to trust God and his Word. When storms come, we must choose to believe that our loving heavenly Father will weave even disasters into the tapestry of our lives in ways that will ultimately bless us and bring him glory. God honors this trust, just as he blessed my trust on the night of the shooting. As I wrestled with my doubts that night, I made the conscious decision to trust him even though I could not imagine how the murders could possibly work for good. I made that choice because his Word, the Bible, tells us he will do just that; and I wanted to believe it, even as I doubted. It took a real act of willpower to make myself trust God in those moments. But that's what he's waiting for: our choosing to trust even when it doesn't make sense.

Once I made that decision, God moved. I chose to forgive everyone who was involved in the murders, but it was God who gave me the power to do so. This may be the biggest lesson for all of us: people hurt other people really badly; but since God commands us to forgive, he will give us his supernatural power to do it if we submit ourselves to him. Even when we feel the task is too big, we can receive help. If we just can't forgive yet, we can pray, "God, help me *want* to forgive"—and before long we'll find that God has worked on our hearts without our realizing it, and we are actually able to extend that forgiveness.

God knows that forgiveness can be the hardest gift for someone to give (and accept), but he also knows it is vital for our own healing—and if we acknowledge our need, in his mercy he will do the heavy lifting. When we give him the reins of our life, he will give us the power to do his will.

By forgiving the faceless strangers who'd hurt me so badly, I was later able to deal with my son when he fell under that very suspicion. The seven months we studied and prayed together before he fled to Mexico were crucial to Bart's eventual healing, but they would have been impossible if I had not already forgiven him. Without forgiveness, I would have remained stuck in my suspicion, bitterness, hurt, and anger, and Bart would have gone to Mexico without experiencing my display of God's unconditional love. He probably would not have made the connection with Christ while there, and he would have returned in shackles to America the same young man who had plotted the murders of his family instead of the new creation he had become. He still would have been Absalom.

And the act of forgiving Bart, Chris, and Steven has healed some of my emotional scars. I am no longer tormented by feelings of conflict with the police. Many times in the last three years, I had thought of the police as the enemy—especially Marshall Slot. All my life I had supported the police and trusted them; but from the day in the hospital when Marshall revealed that Bart had not been enrolled in school, my every connection with the police had resulted in greater and greater disruptions of my life. Until Bart's arrest, I never knew if their warnings were legitimate or just efforts to make him a scape-goat. But now I understand that they were just doing their very unpleasant job, and part of that included forcing me to see that my son's actions were at the root of all my misery.

I had come to understand these truths intellectually months earlier, but it wasn't until after the trial that emotional acceptance came.

It happened one beautiful spring evening when I joined friends from another church for a Friday night Astros game. We were all in great spirits as we climbed higher and higher into the cheap seats, but just as we neared our row, I was surprised to see Marshall, who was making his way toward me.

He had seen me coming and wanted to tell me how much he grieved for what I had been through, and he wanted to know how I was doing. We talked for a few minutes, my heart growing cold as the old fears rose again to the surface, and suddenly I was back in that horrible turmoil. As I struggled with my emotions, Marshall explained that he was with a group of men from his church, and they all had brought their sons with them to the game. Sitting three rows directly above them, I couldn't help but watch Marshall interact with his friends and his young son. He was loving and patient, and everyone was having a great time, as fathers and sons always do at baseball games. I thought about times my dad and I had gone fishing together and to the old Houston Buffs minor league games. I remembered taking Bart and Kevin to baseball games, destruction derbies, football games, and car races, and suddenly I saw that Marshall was really just like me. I realized that the duties of his job had placed the two of us in an impossible situation, but if circumstances had been different, I would have enjoyed having him as a neighbor. We would have felt safe with him next door and knowing that during the day he was protecting all of us. He was just a regular guy.

While I had forgiven Bart, my mind had deflected much of my resentment and anger away from him and placed it where it should not have been. I now felt free of that displaced emotion. When we bumped into each other after the game, Marshall and I shared a Christian hug . . . and I really meant it.

* * *

Long before the shootings took place, I was aware that Bart's favorite movie was *Les Misérables*, the version with Liam Neeson. He watched it often, read the novel by Victor Hugo, and went to the musical. I didn't realize at the time why it affected him so strongly, but now I understand: the hero, Jean Valjean, became the man of virtue that Bart wanted to be. My son identified with the criminal Valjean, the filthy, thieving character of violence who, even though he despised the creature he had become, would still beat up and rob the kind bishop who befriended him. Jean saw his emptiness and imperfection and hated himself, just as Bart did. In the story Jean's soul was rescued by the kind bishop who, through his actions, showed Jean that he was valuable in God's eyes. That redemption is one of the most powerful moments in literature. It is a picture of what Jesus does for us, and although Bart had turned his back on God, somewhere deep inside, he knew the truth: what was wrong with him was only curable by God's love. Bart desperately wanted a Jean Valjean experience.

Bart's life is an extreme example of the need we all have. His story became more public than most, but every one of us has the same need.

The wonder of December 10, 2003, is that it was Bart's version of Jean's theft of the bishop's silver. It launched a series of events that would lead to Bart's restoration with the God who loved him through all of the darkness, even as he wrestled with his inner demons. Bart may have given up on God, but God never gave up on Bart; and he will never give up on you, either. God used all these events to change Bart's heart, bit by bit, just as he changed Jean Valjean's heart in the novel, and just as he changed the prodigal son's heart in the old parable. The good news is that he will do the same in all our lives.

Like in the second half of Blake's poem "The Little Boy Found," God stepped into Bart's life to rescue the lost little boy and lead him back to a loving parent. Bart accepted that forgiveness and was restored.

My Absalom had returned.

Acknowledgments

For two years I fought like a wildcat to keep from writing this book.

Knowing that writing was one of my lifelong hobbies, dozens of friends told me that I should be the one to tell this amazing story. But all I wanted was for the public attention to go away; the last thing in the world I needed was to draw more attention by writing about it. But the media just wouldn't stop. First the shootings, then my son's disappearance, followed by his arrest, leading to his trial and culminating in a national television program: these kept forcing our family's tragedy into the spotlight. Eventually I gave up, opened my eyes, and became convinced that God wanted this story told and he wanted me to tell it.

So here it is, warts and all. I have tried to narrate this so the reader would experience all the feelings I went through, good and bad. Since ultimately this is less a story about a terrible tragedy, and more about how God can take all things (even murder!) and work them for good, it was vital that the reader experience what I experienced. Only then could a stranger truly appreciate how God still works through Life's tragedies,

209

including one this horrible. Only then would he or she be encouraged to look for his help within their own troubles, whatever they might be. God still works.

I had lots of support along the way. Thanks, Dr. Brendan O'Rourke, for helping me see within myself, and for telling me about Glorieta Christian Writers Conference; and thanks DiAnn Mills for your friendship and encouragement. Without both of you this never would have been finished. Much love to you Matt Barnhill, pastor and friend, for keeping me on track when I would start coming unglued emotionally. (You too, Steve Beck and Paul Hicks, my FAT-man buddies!) And Jim Frith, thanks, amigo, for all you did that night, and for the trip to Alaska.

I am grateful to all of you who read and critiqued the work in progress: Helen, Mitch and Brenda G, Bruce, Brenda H, Michele, Fay, Sam, Paul, Robin, Charlene, Carol Ann, Eileen, Lynn, Pam B (Whoa! English grammar lessons at my age!), Pam S, Linda L, Linda G, and my family. And hugs to all of you prayer warriors from coast to coast whom I have never met, but who prayed for Bart and me all those many, many times. Your prayers have been felt and were effective. May God richly bless you for lifting us up.

Much love and special thanks go to my mom and dad, brothers Keith and Don, and my late sister, Nada. I love you and all your families so much. And Bart, I am so grateful that God has restored you. I wish we could have had this relationship all along. I love you, son.

I would also like to give special thanks to Janet Grant of Books and Such Literary Agency, and to Denny Boultinghouse and Susan Wilson of Howard Books for making this process so smooth. You guys are the absolute best.

Even with all the help I received throughout this process, there are probably going to be things that some of you remember a little differently. I guess that is inevitable, but I hope any such discrepancies are small and rare. I have taken the liberty of condensing some conversations because of space constraints, and some quotes may not be exactly word for word with what was actually spoken. I even distilled some long conversations (especially in the trial and between conspirators), but I trust that the spirit and basic content remained accurate. I hope that you will be forgiving if I got the actual words a little wrong here and there; I did not travel this road carrying a tape recorder and I have done the best I could.

One final word: I made the decision long ago that this was going to be God's story, and that his faithfulness, grace, and power were to be its focus. As such, I have chosen to donate all proceeds that I receive for writing this book to charity. I will not personally (nor will my family or friends) be paid anything from your purchase of this book. To that end I have created the December 10 Fund (managed by the Houston Christian Foundation) to receive my royalties. The Fund's directors will coordinate the distribution of all proceeds from the sale of *Murder by Family*.

—Kent Whitaker, March 2008